P9-DYE-954

Practice Book

Grade 3

Harcourt School Publishers

www.harcourtschool.com

Printed in the United States of America

ISBN 10: 0-15-349876-5
ISBN 13: 978-0-15-349876-3

23 0982 15 14
4500469461

Contents

TWISTS AND TURNS

BREAKING NEW GROUND

Name _____

▶ **Read the Spelling Words. Write each word where it belongs.**

Words with Short *a*

1. _____
2. _____
3. _____

Words with Short *e*

4. _____
5. _____
6. _____

Words with Short *i*

7. _____
8. _____
9. _____

Words with Short *o*

10. _____
11. _____
12. _____

Words with Short *u*

13. _____
14. _____
15. _____

Spelling Words

1. this
2. went
3. jump
4. still
5. last
6. dust
7. tell
8. drop
9. shut
10. lamp
11. stop
12. felt
13. drink
14. clock
15. stand

School–Home Connection

Ask your child to help you write a grocery list. Have him or her point out the words that have short vowel sounds and circle the short vowel in each word.

1

Name _____

▶ **Read the story. Then circle the letter of the best answer to each question.**

Maribel and Tracy played in Maribel's grassy backyard nearly every day. Maribel liked to take off her shoes and run barefoot. Tracy always warned her about that. "Watch out," she would say. "You might step on a sharp rock or a piece of glass."

"Don't worry," Maribel would answer. "I will be fine." One day after playing, Maribel put her shoes back on. "Yeow!" she screamed. Maribel's mom came running to help. Quickly, she removed a stinger from Maribel's heel. "There was a bee in your shoe," she told Maribel. Maribel stopped crying for a minute. "See," she said to Tracy. "Running barefoot was safe. It was my shoe that was dangerous!"

1. What is the setting of the story?
   A   the lunch room
   B   Maribel's house
   C   the library
   D   Maribel's yard

> **Tip**
> What words help you tell when and where the action begins?

2. Who is the main character of the story?
   A   Maribel
   B   a teacher
   C   a bee
   D   a pair of shoes

> **Tip**
> Remember that the main character is usually the person who has a problem.

3. Who is another character in the story?
   A   a dog walker
   B   Tracy
   C   Ms. Hamilton
   D   Maribel

> **Tip**
> Remember that another character is someone who interacts with the main character.

School–Home Connection

Have the student select two or three words from the story. Then help him or her to understand what they mean. Together, write a sentence using each word.

2

Name _____

▶ **Read the words in the box. Write each word in the correct column below. You will write some words in more than one column.**

this	went	jump	still	last
dust	tell	drop	shut	lamp
stop	felt	drink	clock	stand

Words that have the letter *t*	Words that have the letter *l*	Words that have the letter *p*
tap	luck	pen
sits	milk	tips
lost	ball	top
1. _____	1. _____	1. _____
2. _____	2. _____	2. _____
3. _____	3. _____	3. _____
4. _____	4. _____	4. _____
5. _____	5. _____	
6. _____	6. _____	
7. _____		
8. _____		
9. _____		
10. _____		

School–Home Connection

Write the following words on a sheet of paper: *past*, *dust*, *doll*, and *pull*. Ask the student which words end in -*st*. Then ask which words end in -*ll*.

3

Practice Book
© Harcourt • Grade 3

Name _____

▶ From the six Vocabulary Words in the box, select the word that best fits with each group of words.

coincidence	pleasant	modeled
murmured	loyal	recited

1. true
   honest
   friend
   _____

2. nice
   smile
   good
   _____

3. same
   not planned
   strange
   _____

4. memorize
   said
   out loud
   _____

5. showed
   taught
   explained
   _____

6. quiet
   said
   shy
   _____

Try This

Say a Vocabulary Word to a few of your classmates. Ask them to share the first words that come into their minds.

School–Home Connection

Have the student name something that he or she has *recited*. Then ask the student to describe a *coincidence* that he or she has experienced.

4

▶ As you read "Ruby the Copycat," fill in the graphic organizer. Each time you come across a new character, write in his or her name. Also, write in each setting. When you have finished, answer the questions that follow.

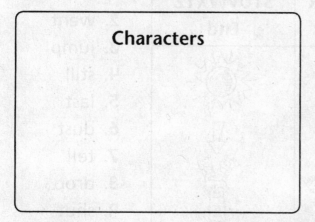

Characters

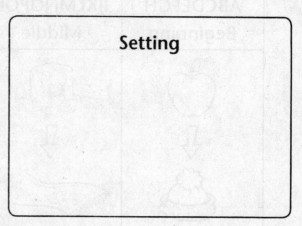

Setting

1. Who is the main character in this story?

   _____

2. Where does most of the story take place?

   _____

3. Who are the other two characters besides the main character?

   _____

4. Where does the story end?

   _____

▶ On a separate sheet of paper, summarize the story. Use the information from the graphic organizer to help you.

Practice Book
© Harcourt • Grade 3

▶ Look at the list of spelling words. Then write each word under the correct part of the alphabet—*beginning, middle,* or *end.*

Spelling Words

1. this
2. went
3. jump
4. still
5. last
6. dust
7. tell
8. drop
9. shut
10. lamp
11. stop
12. felt
13. drink
14. clock
15. stand

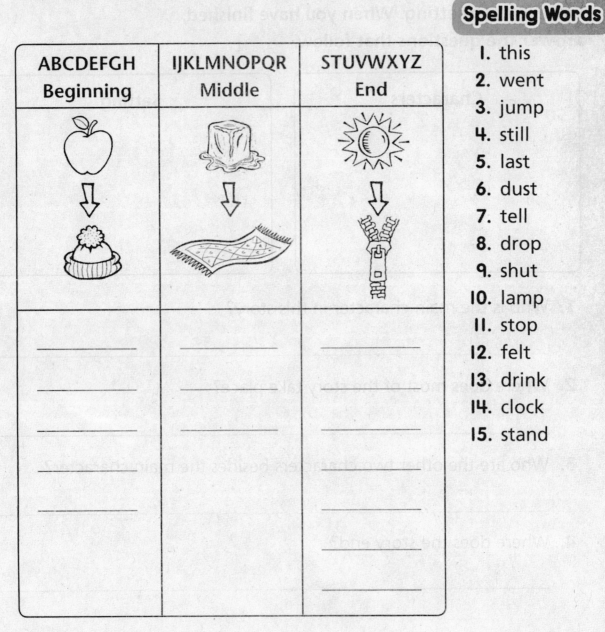

ABCDEFGH Beginning	IJKLMNOPQR Middle	STUVWXYZ End
_____	_____	_____
_____	_____	_____
_____	_____	_____
_____		_____
_____		_____

Practice Book
© Harcourt • Grade 3

► Draw a line from each syllable on the left to a syllable on the right to make a word. Then look across or down in the Search Puzzle to find the words. Circle the words you made.

Syllable Box

1. per   cus
2. sil   cil
3. sis   haps
4. pen   ver
5. cir   ter

Search Puzzle

s	e	l	t	r	o	p	e	r	h	a	p	s
i	p	o	s	i	l	v	e	r	u	z	m	c
s	e	w	i	e	f	n	e	r	k	f	c	l
t	z	c	i	r	c	u	s	v	k	l	o	o
e	n	p	h	f	p	s	s	e	o	p	r	s
r	e	j	x	s	t	u	n	k	p	s	n	g
h	p	e	n	c	i	l	e	d	l	s	e	k
f	m	a	x	s	n	z	l	u	z	p	r	i

School-Home Connection

Review the search words with the student. Discuss their meanings. Then have him or her write a few sentences using some of the words.

7

Practice Book
© Harcourt • Grade 3

Name _____

▶ **Add the correct end mark to each sentence.**
Then label each as a *statement* or a *question*.

1. Where is the teacher _____ _____

2. I do not like to jump _____ _____

3. When does Anita run _____ _____

4. Do you know Mr. Wang _____ _____

5. We play in the grass _____ _____

▶ **Rewrite each group of words to form a statement or a**
question. Put the words in an order that makes sense.
Use capital letters and end marks correctly.

6. to the park I go (statement)

_____

7. do walk you to school (question)

_____

8. Willow ball the throws (statement)

_____

9. can Kurt play softball (statement)

_____

10. you can football play (question)

_____

School–Home Connection

Work with your child to write two questions
about your family and two statements that
answer the questions.

8

Practice Book
© Harcourt • Grade 3

Name _____

▶ **Read the Spelling Words. Write each word where
it belongs.**

Words with -*ed*

1. _____

2. _____

3. _____

4. _____

5. _____

6. _____

7. _____

Words with -*ing*

8. _____

9. _____

10. _____

11. _____

12. _____

13. _____

14. _____

15. _____

Spelling Words

1. saved
2. moved
3. riding
4. waking
5. pulled
6. taking
7. hopped
8. baking
9. picked
10. having
11. letting
12. running
13. drawing
14. folded
15. shopped

School–Home Connection

Help your child make a list of words that
have -*ed* and -*ing* endings. Discuss the correct
spelling for each word. Confirm each word's
spelling with your child, using a dictionary.

9

Practice Book
© Harcourt • Grade 3

▶ **Read the story. Circle the letter of the best answer to each question.**

Marissa wanted to surprise her mother. She was going to paint a picture on a piece of wood. "What color should I use?" she thought.

In a closet, she found pails and pails of paint. There was blue, yellow, red, and every other color she could think of. "I will use every color!" she said to herself. Marissa started to paint. The wet colors mixed together. Her painting was a mess. What could she do?

Just then, her mother came home. Crying, Marissa said, "I wanted to give you a special gift."

Her mother said, "Marissa, your gift *is* special to me. That is because you made it. It looks like a new kind of rainbow! Thank you for your hard work."

Marissa smiled. She helped her mother put the piece of wood on the wall, where they could see it every day.

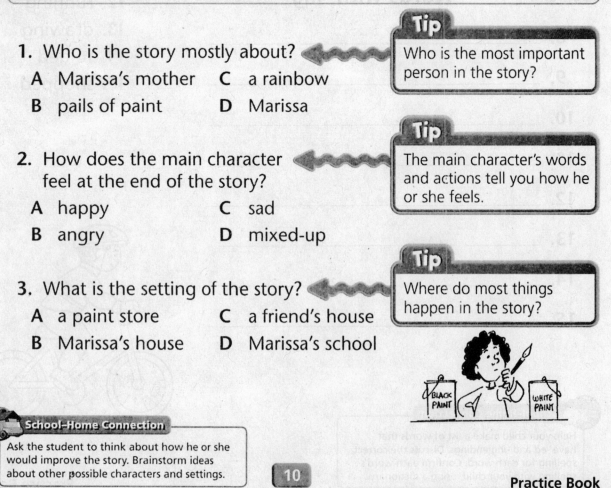

1. Who is the story mostly about?

   A Marissa's mother   C a rainbow

   B pails of paint   D Marissa

   Tip Who is the most important person in the story?

2. How does the main character feel at the end of the story?

   A happy   C sad

   B angry   D mixed-up

   Tip The main character's words and actions tell you how he or she feels.

3. What is the setting of the story?

   A a paint store   C a friend's house

   B Marissa's house D Marissa's school

   Tip Where do most things happen in the story?

School-Home Connection

Ask the student to think about how he or she would improve the story. Brainstorm ideas about other possible characters and settings.

10

Practice Book

© Harcourt • Grade 3

▶ **Read the story, and look at the two columns.**
In the correct column, write the root word for
each underlined verb.

Yesterday afternoon, my mom was <u>driving</u> us home from a family cookout. I <u>stared</u> out the window. "Mom!" I <u>yelled</u>. "There's a gray cat on the road!" My mother <u>braked</u> hard and <u>turned</u> our car to the right. She <u>stopped</u>.

We got out of the car, and the cat <u>walked</u> right up to us. He <u>closed</u> his eyes and <u>purred</u>. I could tell that he <u>liked</u> me a lot. But just then his owner came for him. I told her that I <u>hoped</u> I could have a cat of my own someday.

Roots with Final e	Roots without Final e
_____	_____
_____	_____
_____	_____
_____	_____

School–Home Connection

Write these words on a sheet of paper: *shave*, *tape*, *walk*, and *bend*. Ask the student to add an *-ing* ending to each word. (shaving, taping, walking, bending)

11

Name _____

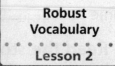
▶ **Read each question and the underlined Vocabulary Word. Write a sentence to answer each question.**

1. If you were going to an <u>assembly</u>, would you expect to see one person or many people?

   _____

2. My little brother <u>squirmed</u> at the doctor's office. Did he sit quietly or did he move around a lot?

   _____

3. If a singer <u>autographed</u> a CD for you, did she sing her name or sign her name?

   _____

4. Mr. Jones will <u>dismiss</u> the class at three o'clock. Do you think a lot of people or no people will be left at three-thirty?

   _____

5. When I make a picture that is a <u>patchwork</u> of color, should I use one color or many colors?

   _____

6. If you brought <u>plenty</u> of food to a picnic, would there be not enough food or more than enough food?

   _____

Try This

Say a Vocabulary Word to a partner. Ask your partner to use it in a sentence.

School–Home Connection

Have the student act out *squirmed* and *autographed*. Ask the student to show how his or her teacher dismisses the class.

12

▶ Fill in the characters, setting, and story events
as you read "The Day Eddie Met the Author."

Section 1 pages 58–59

Characters: Eddie,
_____

Setting:
_____

First: Everyone seems excited about
_____

Next:
_____

Section 2 pages 60–65

Then:
_____

Section 3 pages 66–74

Last:
_____

▶ Use the information in this chart to write a summary of "The Day Eddie
Met the Author." Write your summary on another sheet of paper.

Name _____

► **Put the words from the Spelling Words list in alphabetical order. The first, middle, and last words have been done for you.**

sail
_____
_____
_____
_____
_____

sixty
_____
_____
_____
_____

stick

Spelling Words

1. soap
2. stick
3. sandwich
4. song
5. sock
6. sixteen
7. soup
8. snake
9. smoke
10. sign
11. six
12. salt
13. scarf
14. sixty
15. sail

School–Home Connection

Have the student write two words that begin with the same three letters, like *crate* and *crazy*. Then have him or her write the two words in alphabetical order.

14

Name _____

▶ **Read each root word in the left column. Circle the correct spelling of the word when the ending -ed or -ing is added.**

1. save   saved   saveed

2. hop   hoped   hopped

3. ride   rideing   riding

4. take   taking   takeing

5. dine   dineed   dined

6. let   leting   letting

7. shop   shoped   shopped

8. run   runing   running

9. tip   tipping   tiping

10. wake   waked   wakeed

11. jump   jumpped   jumped

12. step   stepped   steped

13. tell   teling   telling

14. lift   liftting   lifting

15. skip   skipping   skiping

School–Home Connection

Have the student read aloud the words from the list above. Then help him or her write short sentences for five of the words.

15

▶ **If the sentence is complete, add a correct end
mark. If the sentence is not complete, write** *not
a sentence.*

   1. My father is an author _____

   2. How he loves to write _____

   3. How do I help him _____

   4. Things that he can write about _____

   5. Read his latest book _____

   6. Wow, it's exciting _____

▶ **Add words and end marks to make four kinds of sentences.
Each sentence is started for you.**

   7. a statement

      You _____

   8. a command

      Go _____

   9. an exclamation

      What _____

   10. a question

      What _____

School–Home Connection

Work with your child to write a question and a
command about the town where you live. The
command should be related to the question.

16

Practice Book
© Harcourt • Grade 3

Long Vowel
Digraphs /ē/ee,
ea; /ā/ai, ay;
/ō/oa, ow
Lesson 3

Name _____

▶ **Read the Spelling Words. Write each word where it belongs.**

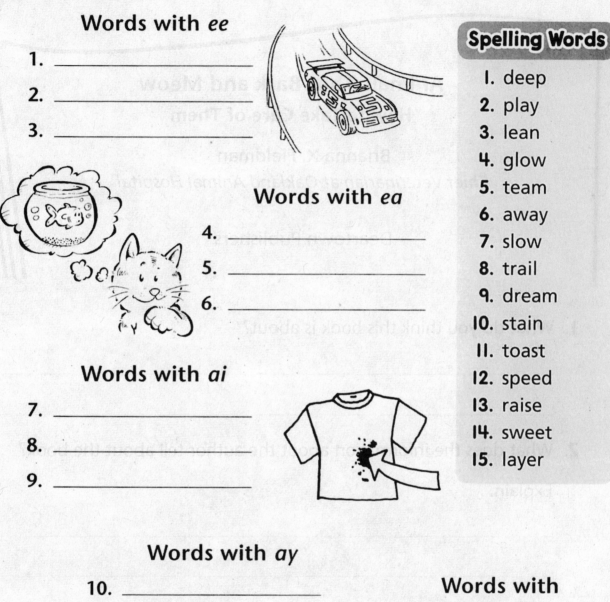

Words with *ee*

1. _____
2. _____
3. _____

Words with *ea*

4. _____
5. _____
6. _____

Words with *ai*

7. _____
8. _____
9. _____

Words with *ay*

10. _____
11. _____
12. _____

Words with *oa* or *ow*

13. _____
14. _____
15. _____

Spelling Words

1. deep
2. play
3. lean
4. glow
5. team
6. away
7. slow
8. trail
9. dream
10. stain
11. toast
12. speed
13. raise
14. sweet
15. layer

School–Home Connection

Work with your child to list words that have long vowel sounds spelled: ee, ea, ai, ay, oa, or ow. Have your child circle the vowels that spell the long vowel sound.

17

▶ **Read the title page below. Then write the answers to the questions.**

Animals That Bark and Meow
How to Take Care of Them

Brianna X. Fieldman
Chief Veterinarian at Oakland Animal Hospital

Deartown Publishers

1. What do you think this book is about?

_____

_____

2. What does the information about the author tell about the book? Explain.

_____

_____

_____

3. What is the name of the publisher?

_____

_____

Name _____

▶ **Read the long /ē/, /ā/ and /ō/ words in the box below. Then complete the paragraph. Write each word where it makes the most sense.**

deep	lean	speed	team	laid	know	row
reach	dream	least	sleep	playing	boat	

Last night, I _____ awake for a while in bed, then I went to

_____ just after 9:00. I had a very strange _____. I was

_____ with some people from my basketball _____. We were

standing on a hill that was at _____ a mile high! When I looked

down, it was like looking into a _____ hole. I didn't _____

why we were there. Then I began to _____ back against a fence,

but I broke right through it! I grabbed for one of my friends, but I

couldn't quite _____ her. Then I began to fall. At first I fell slowly,

but I soon began to _____ toward the ground. Just before I hit the

bottom, I landed in a _____ and began to _____ it up the

river. When I woke up, I found I was in my bed, not on a river, and it was

morning already!

19

Name _____

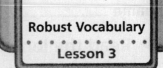

▶ **Answer each question about one of the Vocabulary Words.**

1. If I want a <u>certain</u> book, do I care about which book I get?

_____

_____

2. If you were going to tell me about your family's <u>culture</u>, what is something you could talk about?

_____

_____

3. When you work with a <u>tutor</u>, how will he or she help you?

_____

_____

4. What is an example of <u>chores</u> you do at home?

_____

5. What kind of workers wear <u>uniforms</u>?

_____

6. What are some <u>resources</u> you would need to grow flowers?

_____

_____

Try This

Choose a Vocabulary Word and make up a sentence using the word. Then say the sentence without the Vocabulary Word, and have a partner repeat the sentence with the correct word filled in.

School-Home Connection
Ask the student to write three sentences using the Vocabulary Words on this page.

20

▶ Use the chart to help you organize and locate information from the story "Schools Around the World." Write the title in the first box. Write headings in the boxes just below the title.
Write the main ideas in the boxes under each heading.

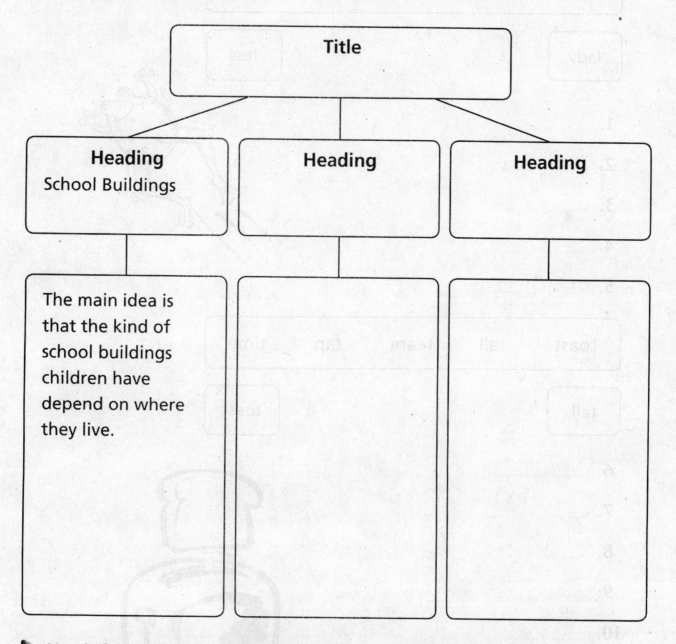

Title

Heading
School Buildings

Heading

Heading

The main idea is that the kind of school buildings children have depend on where they live.

▶ Use information from the chart above to write a summary of the selection on a separate sheet of paper.

▶ **Read the words in each Word Box. Write the words in alphabetical order between the guide words.**

| leap | lean | layer | less | lady |

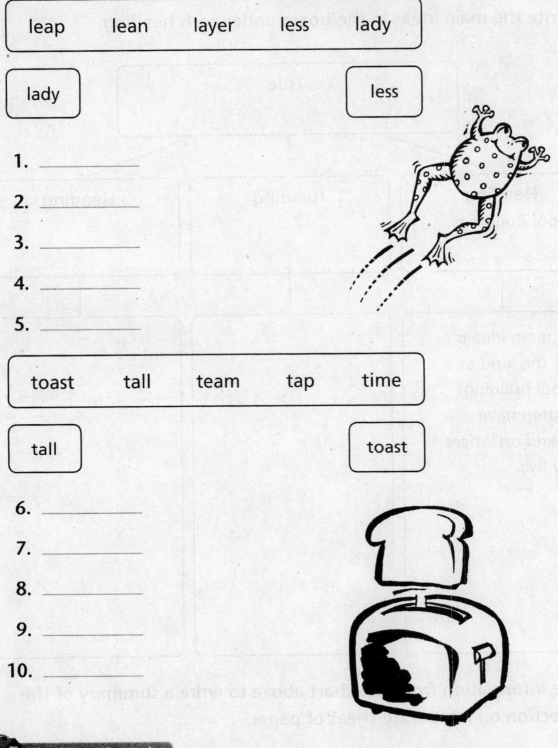

| lady | | less |

1. _____

2. _____

3. _____

4. _____

5. _____

| toast | tall | team | tap | time |

| tall | | toast |

6. _____

7. _____

8. _____

9. _____

10. _____

Practice Book
© Harcourt • Grade 3

Name _____

▶ Read the first word in dark print in each row. Circle another word in the row that has the same vowel sound.

1. **speed**   hen   treat   play

2. **shape**   drain   slow   sheep

3. **grow**   flop   broke   grain

4. **tray**   wade   wide   with

5. **beast**   tree   best   bay

6. **poke**   step   steep   roast

7. **mail**   man   mill   may

8. **oats**   eats   bowl   aims

9. **gray**   spike   cart   face

10. **Pete**   steam   rate   check

School-Home Connection

Have the student think of three words with the long /ā/ sound. Have him or her write the words on a piece of paper and share them with you.

23

Practice Book
© Harcourt • Grade 3

Name _____

▶ **Add a complete subject to each predicate.
Then underline the simple subject.**

1. _____ went to school.

2. _____ played outside.

3. _____ ate lunch.

4. _____ took a nap.

5. _____ performed on stage.

6. _____ was made of brick.

▶ **Add a complete predicate to each subject. Then underline the simple predicate.**

7. An art teacher _____.

8. The excited children _____.

9. He _____.

10. My mother _____.

11. The school _____.

12. The tired baby _____.

Practice Book
© Harcourt • Grade 3

Name _____

▶ **Read the Spelling Words. Write each word where it belongs.**

Base Word with -*s*

1. _____

2. _____

3. _____

4. _____

5. _____

6. _____

Base Word with -*es*

7. _____

8. _____

9. _____

10. _____

11. _____

12. _____

13. _____

14. _____

15. _____

Spelling Words

1. ants
2. toys
3. flies
4. things
5. boxes
6. games
7. lines
8. rocks
9. wishes
10. ladies
11. dishes
12. babies
13. bushes
14. glasses
15. puppies

School–Home Connection

With your child, walk outside and look for groups of plants or objects. Help your child list objects you see, such as bushes, bikes, and houses. Discuss the correct spelling for each word.

25

➤ **Use the Table of Contents to answer the
questions. Write your answers in order on the lines.**

The History of Outer Space
Table of Contents

Chapter   Page

Introduction
1. Why Study Space?. 3
2. Who Studies Space? 8
3. Space in Ancient History. 15
4. Space in the Middle Ages. 24
5. The Space Age. 47

Glossary 58
Index 60

1. What is the title of the fourth chapter?

_____

2. What is the title of the chapter that begins on page 3?

_____

3. On what page would you begin reading "Space in Ancient History"?

_____

4. What is the first page of the Index?

_____

5. What is the title of the second chapter?

_____

School–Home Connection

With the student, brainstorm possible ideas
that might be covered in Chapter 1: "Why
Study Space?"

26

Name _____

▶ **Complete each sentence with the plural form of a word from the box. Be sure to use the correct ending, -s or -es.**

beach	book	box	dime	tree
dress	flash	inch	side	river

1. Shelby tried on three _____ before she found the one she liked best.

2. Florida has some of the most famous sandy _____ in the world.

3. I like to read _____ about outer space.

4. A triangle has three _____.

5. Ms. Green bought two _____ of cereal at the grocery store.

6. I saw some _____ of lightning in the sky last night.

7. A foot is 12 _____ long.

8. One dollar amounts to the same as ten _____.

9. The maple _____ have colorful leaves in the autumn.

10. People can fish in the many _____ that run through the northwest.

School-Home Connection

Ask the student to spell the plural forms of the words in the box without looking at the paper.

27

Practice Book
© Harcourt • Grade 3

▶ **Write the Vocabulary Word from the box that goes with each meaning.**

| apply | disappointed | invention |

1. _____ unhappy about the way things worked out

2. _____ to fill out papers to do something, such as get a job

3. _____ something new that someone makes or creates

▶ **Answer these questions about the Vocabulary Words from the box.**

| talented | research | hinder |

4. What are some things that a talented person might be able to do?

_____

5. What is something you might do research about?

_____

6. If you hinder someone, are you helping her or not helping her?

_____

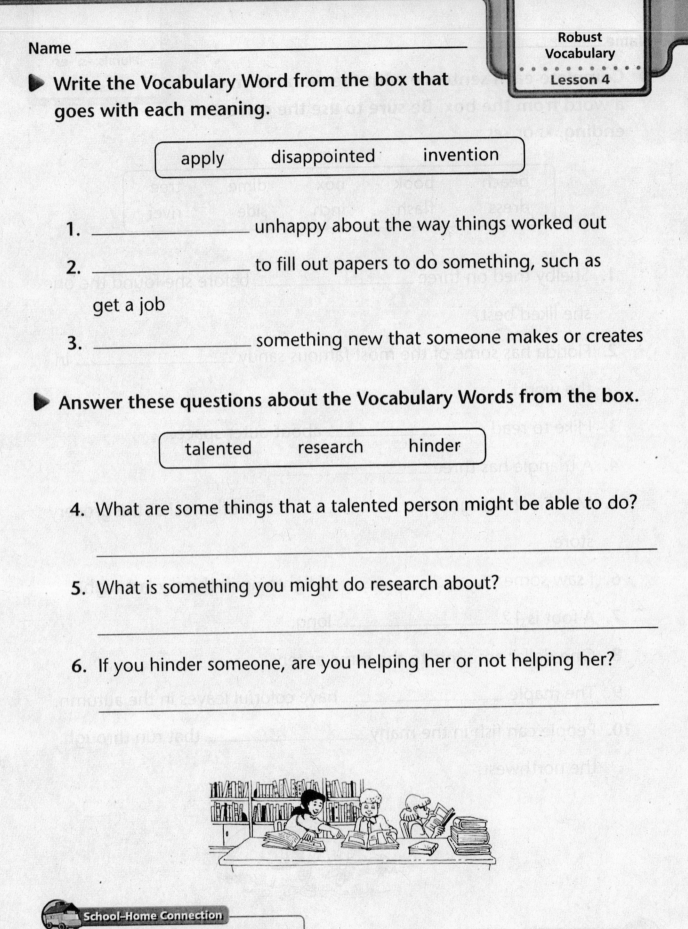

School–Home Connection

With the student, discuss the meanings of any Vocabulary Words that he or she does not understand. Then have the student create a definition for each word.

Practice Book
© Harcourt • Grade 3

▶ As you read "Ellen Ochoa: Astronaut," pay attention to the order in which events are told. Fill in the graphic organizer as you read.

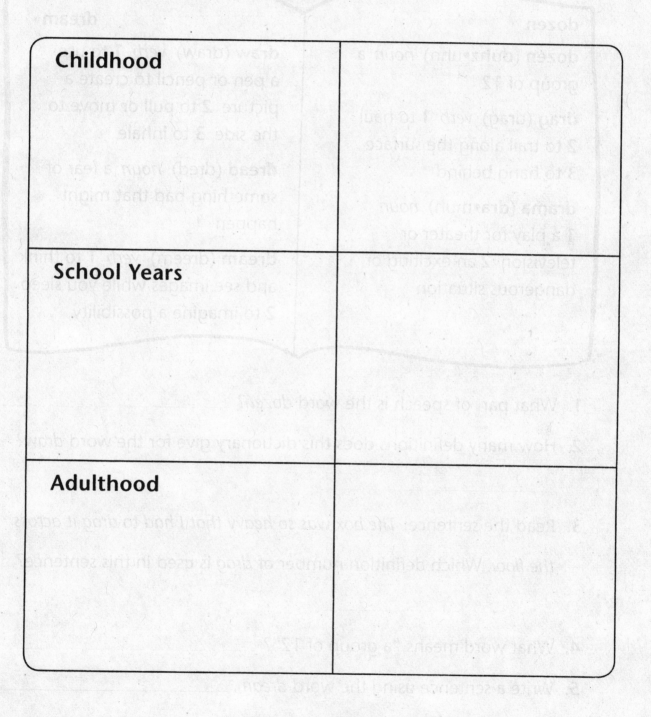

Childhood

School Years

Adulthood

Name _____

▶ **Review the sample dictionary page and answer the questions. Write your answers on the lines.**

---

dozen   **dream**

dozen (**duhz•**uhn) *noun* a group of 12

drag (drag) *verb* **1** to haul **2** to trail along the surface **3** to hang behind

drama (**dra•**muh) *noun* **1** a play for theater or television **2** an exciting or dangerous situation

draw (draw) *verb* **1** to use a pen or pencil to create a picture **2** to pull or move to the side **3** to inhale

dread (dred) *noun* a fear of something bad that might happen

dream (dreem) *verb* **1** to think and see images while you sleep **2** to imagine a possibility

---

1. What part of speech is the word *dozen*? _____

2. How many definitions does this dictionary give for the word *draw*?

   _____

3. Read the sentence: *The box was so heavy that I had to drag it across the floor.* Which definition number of *drag* is used in this sentence?

   _____

4. What word means "a group of 12"? _____

5. Write a sentence using the word *dream*. _____

   _____

School-Home Connection

Have the student pronounce all six words and use each one in a sentence.

30

Practice Book
© Harcourt • Grade 3

Name _____

▶ **Write the plural form of each noun. Then circle the plural words in the Word Search.**

1. country _____

2. cage _____

3. story _____

4. lunch _____

5. tree _____

6. fork _____

7. tray _____

8. party _____

9. set _____

10. book _____

Word Search

```
B D T R N W A F O R K E S L H
W C A Y Z E C O U N T R I E S
T R E E S L M R W Q I P Z B T
R G S A A C I K U P F C C O O
A S D D P Q A S L E O A H O R
Y E Y P A R T I E S D G U K I
S T O R Y S T E D A E E A S E
E S L L U N C H E S S S M I S
```

Practice Book
© Harcourt • Grade 3

Name _____

▶ **Add a compound subject or a compound predicate to complete each sentence.**

1. _____ studied art.

2. The athletes _____.

3. The music student _____.

4. _____ took dance classes.

5. The actor _____.

6. _____ watched the stars.

▶ **Rewrite each sentence. Add commas where they belong. Draw one line under each compound subject and two lines under each compound predicate.**

7. The soccer player ran kicked and scored.

_____

8. Exercise rest and healthful food made the swimmer strong.

_____

_____

9. Raja his sister and his brother were good students.

_____

10. The scientist wrote a book won a prize and gave a speech.

_____

_____

School–Home Connection

Work with your child to write one sentence
about his or her day using a compound subject
and one sentence using a compound predicate.

32

Practice Book
© Harcourt • Grade 3

Name _____

▶ **Part A. Read the sentences. Find one CVC
word and one VCCV word in each sentence.
Write the words in the spaces below each sentence.**

1. Rihanna's dog is such a rascal!

   CVC: _____   VCCV: _____

2. Hilary drew a beautiful picture on the wooden box.

   CVC: _____   VCCV: _____

3. The runner wore a baseball cap during the race.

   CVC: _____   VCCV: _____

4. Just give the ball a tap with the racket.

   CVC: _____   VCCV: _____

5. There is rubber cement in the den.

   CVC: _____   VCCV: _____

▶ **Part B. Choose one CVC word and one VCCV word from Part A,
and write a short story using both words.**

_____

_____

_____

_____

_____

School–Home Connection

Ask the student to find the short vowel sounds
in *racket* and *rubber*.

33

Name _____

▶ **Fold the paper along the dotted line. As each spelling word is read aloud, write it in the blank. Then unfold your paper and check your work. Practice writing any spelling words you missed.**

1. _____

2. _____

3. _____

4. _____

5. _____

6. _____

7. _____

8. _____

9. _____

10. _____

11. _____

12. _____

13. _____

14. _____

15. _____

Spelling Words

1. clock
2. drink
3. hopped
4. moved
5. waking
6. folded
7. stain
8. layer
9. team
10. slow
11. toast
12. ladies
13. flies
14. bushes
15. games

Name _____

▶ **Read the story. Write the root word for each underlined word in the correct column below the story.**

Yesterday afternoon, I was <u>feeling</u> a little bored. I sat and <u>looked</u> out our front window, <u>waiting</u> for something to happen.

As I was <u>staring</u> down the street, a boy skipped by with the strangest dog I had ever seen. I went outside, <u>closing</u> the door behind me.

The boy turned and <u>faced</u> me. "This is Twinkletoes," he said. "We have a big show tomorrow."

I <u>glanced</u> again at his pet. "Is it a dog show?" I asked.

Just then, Twinkletoes oinked. "Oh, no," said the boy. "It is a show at the State Fair. Twinkletoes is a pig!"

As Twinkletoes and the boy <u>walked</u> down the street, I was sorry for thinking my street was boring!

Root Words with Final *e*

_____

_____

_____

_____

Root Words without Final *e*

_____

_____

_____

_____

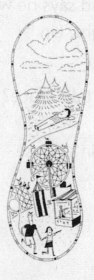

School–Home Connection

Ask the student to identify the root words in *skipped, turned,* and *thinking.*

Practice Book
© Harcourt • Grade 3

▶ **Read the story. Circle the letter of the best answer to each question.**

> Lin's father was working very hard to open a new restaurant. He was nervous and very grouchy. One day, Lin decided to cheer him up. She sneaked into the restaurant with a handful of flowers she had picked. She said to herself, "These will look pretty on the tables. They will make Dad happy."
>
> That night at bedtime, Lin's father came to say good night. "Sleep tight, Lin," he said. He turned off the lights and started to close the door.
>
> "Good night, Dad," she said. She was disappointed that he had not noticed the flowers. Then her father turned the lights back on. "I almost forgot," he said, pulling a flower from his shirt pocket and smiling. "I will make a big breakfast for us in the morning!"

1. Who are the characters in this story?
    A Lin and her mother
    B a father and son
    C Lin and her father

2. How can you tell that Lin's father is happy at the end of the story?
    A He smiles at Lin and says he will make her a big breakfast.
    B He says "Good night, Lin."
    C He is always sad.

3. Where does the story take place?
    A a movie theater
    B a restaurant and Lin's house
    C a friend's house

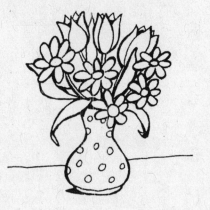

School–Home Connection

Have the student describe Lin and explain how
he or she knows what Lin is like.

36

Practice Book
© Harcourt • Grade 3

▶ **Read this part of a student's rough draft.
Then answer the questions that follow.**

> (1) There is something new in Room 112 (2) Can you guess what it is (3) our rabbit has four babies. (4) How tiny the bunnies are! (5) Wish could take one home. (6) Do you bunnies like?

1. Which sentence should end with a period?

   A Sentence 1

   B Sentence 2

   C Sentence 4

   D Sentence 6

2. Which sentence should end with a question mark?

   A Sentence 1

   B Sentence 2

   C Sentence 3

   D Sentence 4

3. In which sentence are the words in an order that does not make sense?

   A Sentence 2

   B Sentence 3

   C Sentence 4

   D Sentence 6

4. Which word in Sentence 3 should be capitalized?

   A our

   B rabbit

   C four

   D babies

5. Which of the following is NOT a complete sentence?

   A Sentence 1

   B Sentence 3

   C Sentence 4

   D Sentence 5

6. Which sentence is correct as it is?

   A Sentence 3

   B Sentence 4

   C Sentence 5

   D Sentence 6

Practice Book
© Harcourt • Grade 3

Name _____

Review Vowel
Digraphs: ee, ea,
ai, ay, oa, ow
Lesson 5

▶ **Underline the letters that make the long vowel sound in each word. Then circle the word whose vowel sound is different from the other two in the line.**

1. bait   freeze   away

2. treat   feed   goal

3. essay   throw   goat

4. crow   drain   tray

5. mean   complain   see

6. snow   bowl   beak

7. reach   delay   feel

8. way   raise   beep

9. seal   coast   teeth

10. heap   know   oat

38

Practice Book
© Harcourt • Grade 3

Name _____

▶ **Complete the sentences below by putting the words in ( ) in alphabetical order and writing them in the blanks.**

1. To compete in that race, you must be able to _____

   five miles, _____ two miles, and _____

   500 feet. (swim, bike, run)

2. Maxine puts her _____ on her bed and leaves her

   _____ in the _____.

   (garage, football, doll)

3. For dinner last night, we had _____ with a side of

   _____ and _____.

   (peas, potatoes, chicken)

4. Austin keeps his _____ in a _____

   outdoors, but his _____ lives in the house.

   (bunny, cat, cage)

5. There were _____ and _____ on the

   nature show, but there were no _____.

   (lizards, leopards, lions)

6. You should travel by _____ or _____

   to get to Alaska from Florida. It is very far to travel there by

   _____. (truck, train, plane)

School–Home Connection

Together, write the names of five people the student knows. Have him or her put the names in alphabetical order.

Practice Book
© Harcourt • Grade 3

▶ **Part A. Read the sentences below. Fill in the blanks with one of the Vocabulary Words from the Word Box.**

viewers	concealed	survive
independent	camouflage	donated

1. When I taught myself how to tie my shoes, I felt

_____.

2. Rico and Nate looked for bugs in their backyard. They checked

under the log to see if any were _____ there.

3. That television show is so funny! I am sure it has lots of

_____.

4. When Brenda outgrew her jacket, her mom

_____ it to the thrift store.

5. A cactus can _____ without much water.

6. Claire used a pile of laundry as _____ when she

hid in her messy bedroom.

▶ **Part B. Write one sentence that uses any two Vocabulary Words from above.**

_____

_____

40

▶ **Change the underlined noun to its plural form so that the sentence is correct. Write the new word on the line.**

1. I found a basket of <u>kitten</u> on the sidewalk.

   _____

2. Murat loves to collect <u>butterfly</u>. _____

3. There are four different juice <u>mix</u> in our pantry.

   _____

4. Brodie has three <u>wrench</u> in his tool kit. _____

5. The workers built the shed with hammers and <u>nail</u>.

   _____

6. Martina blows <u>kiss</u> to her friends as she gets on the bus.

   _____

7. Everyone in the class gave <u>speech</u> yesterday.

   _____

8. Why do you think clowns have red <u>nose</u>? _____

9. It is good to give <u>flower</u> water and sunlight.

   _____

10. Carol carries two <u>suitcase</u> when she travels overseas.

    _____

School–Home Connection
Ask the student to say the plural form of the nouns *activity*, *princess*, and *group*.

41

Practice Book
© Harcourt • Grade 3

▶ **Read this part of a student's rough draft.
Then answer the questions that follow.**

> (1) Eric watched the news on TV. (2) His father watched the news on TV. (3) The newscaster talked about special events. (4) A police officer a firefighter and a teacher taught third graders about safety. (5) The mayor took a trip and gave a speech.

1. Which is the simple subject of Sentence 1?

   A Eric

   B Eric watched

   C the news

   D watched the news on TV

2. Which is the complete predicate of Sentence 3?

   A the newscaster

   B the newscaster talked

   C talked

   D talked about special events

3. What is missing in Sentence 4?

   A commas

   B a subject

   C a simple predicate

   D a complete predicate

4. Which sentence has a compound subject?

   A Sentence 1

   B Sentence 3

   C Sentence 4

   D Sentence 5

5. Which sentence has a compound predicate?

   A Sentence 2

   B Sentence 3

   C Sentence 4

   D Sentence 5

6. Which sentences could be joined to make one sentence with a compound subject?

   A Sentences 1 and 2

   B Sentences 2 and 3

   C Sentences 3 and 4

   D Sentences 4 and 5

▶ Use your *Student Edition* to answer the questions.
Write the answers on the lines.

1. Turn to page 22 and look at the illustration. What do you think

   is happening?

   _____

2. Turn to the table of contents. On which page does "The Singing

   Marvel" begin?

   _____

3. Turn to page 89 and look at the photographs on the page. What do

   you think this page will be about?

   _____

4. Turn to page 106 and look at the illustrations. What do you think

   the story is about?

   _____

5. Turn to page 116 and look at the title. What do you think this

   selection is about?

   _____

6. What is the last page of the story, "Ellen Ochoa, Astronaut"?

   _____

School–Home Connection

Ask the student to look at the picture on
the cover of the *Student Edition* and write a
possible caption for it.

43

Name _____

► **Review the sample dictionary page and answer the questions.**

chase • cider

chase (chās) *verb* **1** to follow in order to catch someone or something. *noun* **2** the act of chasing.

cheap (chēp) *adjective* **1** low in cost, inexpensive. **2** of poor quality.

chick (chik) *noun* **1** a young chicken. *noun* **2** any young bird.

choose (chōōz) *verb* **1** to select. *verb* **2** to prefer (to do something).

cider (si′dər) *noun* **1** juice pressed from fruits, usually apples.

1. What part of speech is the word *chick*? _____

2. How many definitions does this dictionary give for the word

   choose? _____

3. Which definition of *cheap* is used in the following sentence?

   These comic books are cheap, so I will buy three of

   them. _____

4. How many syllables does *cider* have? _____

5. Which word can be a verb or a noun? _____

6. Which word has only one possible definition? _____

44

Name _____

▶ **Make cards for the Spelling Words. Lay them down and read them.**

   1. Put the words with *up* in the first column.

   2. Put the words with *room* in the second column.

The first one is done for you.

Words with *up*	Words with *room*
1. **pickup**	3. _____
2. _____	4. _____

Words without *up* or *room*

5. _____

6. _____

7. _____

8. _____

9. _____

10. _____

11. _____

12. _____

13. _____

14. _____

15. _____

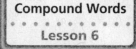

Spelling Words

1. pickup
2. cannot
3. outside
4. bedroom
5. upstairs
6. raindrop
7. baseball
8. hallway
9. airplane
10. mailbox
11. sunshine
12. homework
13. classroom
14. something
15. playground

School–Home Connection

With your child, make a list of compound words. Write the words on a sheet of paper. Talk about the two smaller words that make up each compound word.

Practice Book
© Harcourt • Grade 3

Name _____

▶ **Read the passage. Then circle the letter of the best answer to each question.**

> The Sunshine Skyway Bridge in Florida was finished in 1987. Many people believe it is the most beautiful bridge in the world. It is painted yellow. I think the color is the reason that the bridge is so popular.
>
> Another bridge once stood over Tampa Bay. Because of a terrible storm, 1,000 feet of that bridge fell into the bay. The Sunshine Skyway Bridge is 190 feet above the water at its highest point. It is held together by steel cables.
>
> I feel that this bridge is the strongest bridge of all.

1. Which of the following sentences states a fact?
   - A   It is painted yellow.
   - B   I think the color is the reason that the bridge is so popular.
   - C   Many people believe it is the most beautiful bridge in the world.
   - D   I feel that this bridge is the strongest bridge of all.

2. Which of the following sentences is an opinion?
   - A   The Sunshine Skyway Bridge in Florida was finished in 1987.
   - B   I think the color is the reason that the bridge is so popular.
   - C   Another bridge once stood over Tampa Bay.
   - D   It is held together by steel cables.

3. Read the underlined sentence in the passage. It is a fact. How do you know?
   - A   It is the author's belief.
   - B   It is incorrect information.
   - C   It is something that can be seen or proved.
   - D   All bridges do this.

46

Practice Book
© Harcourt • Grade 3

▶ **Find and circle the ten compound words in the story. Write each one in the box below the story. Use a line to separate the compound word into two smaller words.**

My Vacation

This summer, my family visited a waterside cottage at the beach. We could watch oceangoing steamships pass right by. I spent hours exploring the beach, and I found dozens of beautiful seashells.

Mom took sunrise walks every day, while my brother tried to ride a surfboard. He did not get very far! Dad spent time in a rowboat. He would drop his line into the water and wait for the fish to bite.

We only stayed indoors during thunderstorms. Then we would just watch the lightning, listen to the thunder, and wait to go outside again.

47

Name _____

▶ **Choose a Vocabulary Word to complete each sentence. Write the word on the line.**

collapses	dazed	elevated
embarrass	midst	shabby

1. Maya was in the _____ of a large crowd of people.

2. The _____ shirt was too old to wear any longer.

3. Alejandro felt _____ after the ball hit his head.

4. The television was _____ so that everyone could watch it.

5. Do kind words and compliments _____ you?

6. Someone should repair that building before it _____.

▶ **Find a Vocabulary Word in the box below with a meaning that matches the set of three words. Write the Vocabulary Word on the line.**

collapses	dazed	elevated
embarrass	midst	shabby

7. confused   foggy   dazzled   _____

8. raised   top   high   _____

9. topples   crashes   falls   _____

10. ragged   torn   old   _____

11. center   core   middle   _____

12. shame   disgrace   upset   _____

48

▶ Use the graphic organizer to record the facts and opinions from these pages of "The Babe and I." Write each fact in the column labeled **Fact**. Write each opinion in the column labeled **Opinion**.

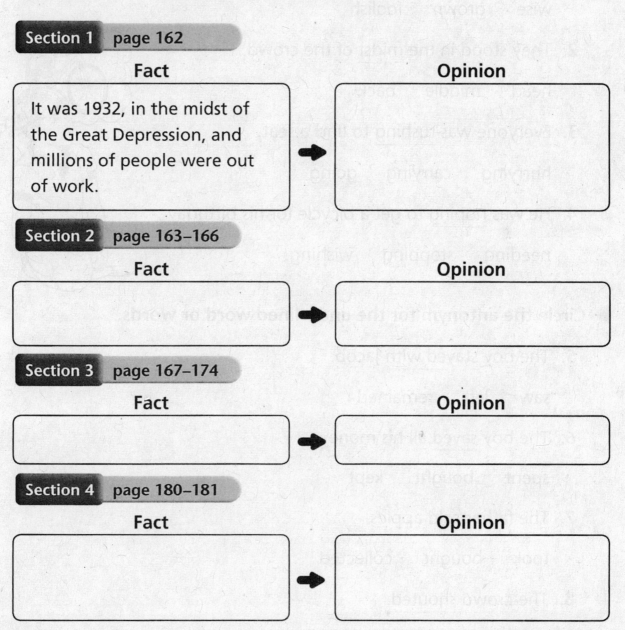

Section 1 page 162

Fact

It was 1932, in the midst of the Great Depression, and millions of people were out of work.

Opinion

Section 2 page 163–166

Fact

Opinion

Section 3 page 167–174

Fact

Opinion

Section 4 page 180–181

Fact

Opinion

▶ On a separate sheet of paper, summarize the story with three facts and three opinions. Use the graphic organizer to help you.

Practice Book
© Harcourt • Grade 3

Name _____

▶ **Read each sentence and the words under it.**
Circle the synonym for the underlined word.

1. He was <u>smart</u> enough to wait for his father.

   wise   grown   foolish

2. They stood in the <u>midst</u> of the crowd.

   head   middle   back

3. Everyone was <u>rushing</u> to find a seat.

   hurrying   carrying   going

4. He was <u>hoping</u> to get a bicycle for his birthday

   needing   stopping   wishing

▶ **Circle the antonym for the underlined word or words.**

5. The boy <u>stayed</u> with Jacob.

   saw   left   remained

6. The boy <u>saved</u> all his money.

   spent   bought   kept

7. The father <u>sold</u> apples.

   took   bought   collected

8. The crowd <u>shouted</u>.

   whispered   yelled   cheered

School-Home Connection
Have the student write antonyms for questions
1-4 and synonyms for questions 5-8.

Practice Book
© Harcourt • Grade 3

Name _____

▶ **Connect each word in the left column with a
word in the right column, to form a compound
word. Then, write a sentence using each compound
word.**

apple   hook

down   case

coat   storm

thunder   hill

suit   sauce

1. _____

_____

2. _____

_____

3. _____

_____

4. _____

_____

5. _____

_____

School–Home Connection

Have the student read his or her sentences
aloud. Discuss the meaning of each compound
word.

51

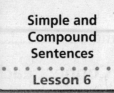
▶ **Rewrite the sentences. Use commas and joining words correctly.**

1. My father is a teacher and he works at a school.

   _____

2. He drives to work, he takes a bus.

   _____

3. He has lunch at work or he eats in the park.

   _____

4. Most days he eats tuna, today he eats egg salad.

   _____

▶ **Rewrite each pair of sentences as one sentence. Use commas and the joining words *and* or *but* correctly.**

5. Mrs. Lopez loves to read. She owns a bookstore.

   _____

6. The store is small. It has many books.

   _____

7. Sasha works with animals. She enjoys her job.

   _____

8. She lives in the country. She works in the city.

   _____

School–Home Connection

Work with your child to write two simple
sentences about a person and his or her job.
Then help your child turn the sentences into
one compound sentence.

Practice Book
© Harcourt • Grade 3

Name _____

▶ **Read the Spelling Words. Find the consonants ch, tch, sh, or wh in each word. Write each word below where it belongs.**

ch, wh, sh at the Beginning

1. _____
2. _____
3. _____
4. _____
5. _____
6. _____
7. _____
8. _____

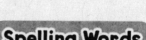

Spelling Words

1. chin
2. itch
3. push
4. chef
5. when
6. wash
7. much
8. sharp
9. pitch
10. where
11. peach
12. child
13. wheat
14. chance
15. machine

ch in the Middle

9. _____

sh, ch, tch at the End

10. _____
11. _____
12. _____
13. _____
14. _____
15. _____

School–Home Connection

Challenge your child to write as many words with the consonant digraphs sh, wh, ch, and tch as possible. Confirm each spelling with your child by using a print or online dictionary.

53

Practice Book
© Harcourt • Grade 3

▶ **Read the passage below. Then answer the questions that follow.**

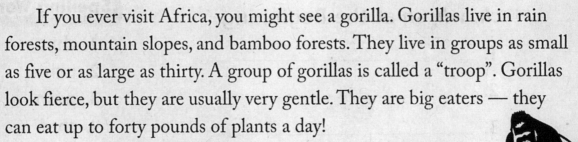

If you ever visit Africa, you might see a gorilla. Gorillas live in rain forests, mountain slopes, and bamboo forests. They live in groups as small as five or as large as thirty. A group of gorillas is called a "troop". Gorillas look fierce, but they are usually very gentle. They are big eaters — they can eat up to forty pounds of plants a day!

Sadly, gorillas are in danger. Logging companies cut down forests where gorillas live, leaving them homeless. It is sad to imagine gorillas with no place to live. Some people are trying to create new wildlife laws to protect gorillas. It is hard work, but saving gorillas is an important cause.

1. What is one opinion from the passage?

_____

_____

2. What is one fact from the passage?

_____

_____

3. What is another opinion from the passage?

_____

_____

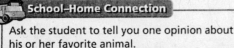

School–Home Connection

Ask the student to tell you one opinion about his or her favorite animal.

Practice Book
© Harcourt • Grade 3

▶ **Complete each sentence with a /ch/ word
spelled *ch* or *tch*. Write the word on the line.
See the word box if you need help.**

chance	watch	peach	hatched
bench	chin	pitch	children

1. Something you wear on your wrist that tells time is a _____.

    _____

2. If you have a group of more than one young person, you have a

    group of _____.

    _____

3. When the bird came out of the egg, the egg was _____.

    _____

4. In a baseball game, you _____ the ball to the batter.

    _____

5. You may want to sit on the park _____ and rest a while.

    _____

6. A fuzzy fruit that grows on trees is a _____.

    _____

7. An opportunity is a _____ you take.

    _____

8. The part of your face just below your mouth is your _____.

    _____

55

▶ **Read each question, paying special attention
to the Vocabulary Word in dark type. Then circle
the letter of the best answer.**

1. How can a dog **obey** its owner?
   A By following the owner's commands
   B By doing the opposite of what the owner asks
   C By barking at other dogs

2. What sound would a child make if he or she **whined**?
   A A happy sound
   B A complaining sound
   C A playful sound

3. What can give off a pleasant **scent**?
   A A skunk
   B A pile of garbage
   C A bed of flowers

4. How can you **demonstrate** the way to set a table?
   A Tell someone what to do.
   B Ask someone to show you how to do it.
   C Do it yourself while someone is watching.

5. What does someone do who **wanders** about?
   A Walks without a plan
   B Talks on the phone for hours
   C Writes a long letter

6. Why would someone **patrol** a neighborhood?
   A To water the plants
   B To keep it safe
   C To keep it crowded

School–Home Connection
Have the student use each Vocabulary Word in
an original sentence.

Practice Book
© Harcourt • Grade 3

Name _____

▶ As you read "Aero and Officer Mike," fill in the graphic organizer with facts and opinions from the passage.

Section 1	pages 200–209

Fact	Opinion
• Aero is a black and tan German shepherd.	

Section 2	pages 210–215

1. What is a fact about Aero's training?

_____

_____

2. How does Aero feel about steep stairs and open gratings?

_____

▶ On a separate sheet of paper, summarize the selection. Use the graphic organizer to help you.

► **Write a synonym or antonym for the underlined word in each sentence.**

1. Kim had to <u>jump</u> to reach the top shelf of her closet.

   Synonym: _____

2. I cannot see <u>over</u> the table from where I am sitting.

   Antonym: _____

3. Joe thought that last night's show was <u>awful</u>.

   Synonym: _____

4. You can keep any of the <u>objects</u> in this box.

   Synonym: _____

5. Those books are <u>heavy</u>.

   Antonym: _____

6. The ranger's cabin is in the <u>woods</u>.

   Synonym: _____

7. <u>Everybody</u> wants to go to the movies tonight.

   Antonym: _____

8. The dog's <u>hair</u> is brown.

   Synonym: _____

Consonant
Digraphs: *ch, sh,
(h)w, wh*

Lesson 7

Name _____

▶ **Circle the word with the consonant pattern
that is not pronounced like the other two.**

1. chin   march   chef

2. when   why   who

3. chubby   cash   machine

4. child   sharp   chance

5. write   wrist   wheat

6. push   pitch   chap

7. shake   shoot   chase

8. stitch   whale   catch

9. much   patch   wheel

10. short   chat   chart

School–Home Connection

With the student, write four sentences that
use at least one word each with consonant
patterns *ch*, *tch*, *sh*, and *wh*.

59

Practice Book
© Harcourt • Grade 3

▶ **Rewrite each sentence correctly.**

1. danny has a Partner in the classroom.

   _____

2. Her Name is ann.

   _____

3. Danny and ann study every Afternoon.

   _____

4. On fridays the Children learn math.

   _____

▶ **Rewrite each sentence correctly. Underline the common nouns. Circle the proper nouns.**

5. Independence day was on tuesday.

   _____

6. Yani's class went to new york city and saw fireworks.

   _____

7. Lights filled the sky over the hudson river.

   _____

8. The Students wrote a report about their trip.

   _____

School–Home Connection

Work with your child to name a proper noun
for each of the following common nouns:
teacher, friend, place, day, month, holiday.

60

Name _____

Vowel Diphthongs
/ou/ou, ow;
/oi/oi, oy

Lesson 8

▶ **Read the Spelling Words. Write each word where it belongs.**

Words with *ou*

1. _____
2. _____
3. _____
4. _____
5. _____

Words with *ow*

6. _____
7. _____
8. _____
9. _____

Spelling Words

1. foil
2. loud
3. gown
4. coil
5. house
6. annoy
7. growl
8. moist
9. enjoy
10. round
11. spoil
12. mouse
13. clown
14. bounce
15. cowboy

Words with *oi*

10. _____
11. _____
12. _____
13. _____

Words with *oy*

14. _____
15. _____
16. _____

School–Home Connection

Help your child write a sentence using each
Spelling Word. Then have him or her circle the
vowels that spell the /oi/ sound.

61

Name _____

▶ **Read the paragraph. Then follow the directions and answer the questions below.**

> Did you know that rabbits eat only plants? This type of animal is called a herbivore. Animals that are carnivores, like tigers, eat only meat. Some animals, like bears, eat both plants and meat. They are called omnivores. An animal can be a herbivore, carnivore, or omnivore depending on what it eats.

1. Write the main idea. _____

_____

_____

2. Draw a box around each of the supporting details.

3. Write the main idea in a different way so that you could put it at the beginning of the paragraph. _____

_____

_____

School–Home Connection

Have the student tell you in his or her own words what the paragraph is about. Explain to the student that this is the main idea.

Practice Book
© Harcourt • Grade 3

▶ **Find ten spelling words in the Word Search puzzle that have the vowel sound /ou/ and /oi/. The words go across or down. Circle the words and write a sentence for each one.**

Word Search

C	H	L	O	U	D	T	A	N	N	O	Y
R	W	N	D	G	W	O	O	C	Y	F	L
O	Q	K	H	O	U	S	E	Z	T	O	C
U	G	R	O	W	L	X	R	U	Q	I	O
N	P	C	M	N	O	Y	X	L	X	L	I
D	C	L	O	W	N	O	S	P	O	I	L

1. _____

2. _____

3. _____

4. _____

5. _____

6. _____

7. _____

8. _____

9. _____

10. _____

School–Home Connection

On a sheet of paper, work with the student to write five more words with the sound /ou/ as in *mouse*.

Practice Book
© Harcourt • Grade 3

Name _____

▶ **Part A. Write the Vocabulary Word from the Word Box that matches each idea.**

communicate	flick	alert
signal	chatter	grooms

1. _____ to make neat and clean

2. _____ to tell a person or animal something

3. _____ to warn someone

4. _____ to make noises over and over

5. _____ a movement that has a meaning

6. _____ to snap something quickly

▶ **Part B. Use what you know about the Vocabulary Words to answer each question. Answer in complete sentences.**

7. If you **alert** someone, are you smiling at the person or warning the person? _____

8. If you **flick** a towel, does the towel move quickly or slowly?

   _____

9. If a person **grooms** his dog, is he brushing it or feeding it?

   _____

10. If you **chatter** with a friend, are you speaking quickly or whispering?

    _____

11. When you give someone a **signal**, what are you doing?

    _____

12. Do you **communicate** by yourself or with other people?

    _____

School-Home Connection
Have the student act out the words *alert* and *chatter*. Then use your hands to send a *signal* to him or her. Have the student guess what the signal means.

Practice Book
© Harcourt • Grade 3

Name _____

▶ As you read "How Animals Talk," fill in the graphic organizer with important details from the selection. Then write the most important idea from the selection.

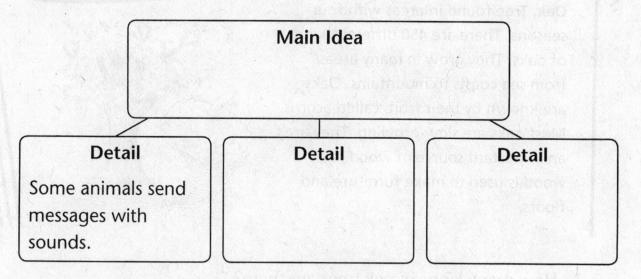

Main Idea

Detail
Some animals send messages with sounds.

Detail

Detail

1. What is the main idea of the selection?

_____

_____

_____

_____

2. What are three of the most important details?

_____

_____

_____

▶ On a separate sheet of paper, summarize the selection. Use the graphic organizer to help you.

65

▶ **Read the encyclopedia entry. Use the information to answer the questions.**

Oak. Tree found in areas with four seasons. There are 450 different kinds of oaks. They grow in many areas, from sea coasts to mountains. Oaks are known by their fruit, called acorns. Most oaks are slow-growing. They are an important source of wood. Oak wood is used to make furniture and floors.

1. How many kinds of oak trees are there?

_____

2. What is oak wood used to make?

_____

3. What is an acorn?

_____

4. What are two of the areas in which oaks grow?

_____

5. Where are oak trees found?

_____

School-Home Connection

Help the student write a poem about oak trees and acorns. Then read it aloud together.

66

Practice Book
© Harcourt • Grade 3

Name _____

▶ **Unscramble the words. Each word includes the letter pattern *ou, ow, oi,* or *oy*. Then use each word in a sentence.**

1. wodn ➡ _____

   _____

2. liob ➡ _____

   _____

3. tipon ➡ _____

   _____

4. yots ➡ _____

   _____

5. lowh ➡ _____

   _____

6. hotum ➡ _____

   _____

7. dolu ➡ _____

   _____

8. rewot ➡ _____

   _____

School–Home Connection

Write the letters *thuso* on a sheet of paper.
Have the student unscramble them to form a
word that uses one of the letter patterns above.

67

Name _____

▶ **Write the full word for each abbreviation.**

1. FL _____

2. Tues. _____

3. Dr. _____

4. St. _____

5. Apr. _____

▶ **Find the words in each sentence that have abbreviations. Write the abbreviations.**

6. Mister Ward's party is on Sunday, November 5.

_____

7. Send the letter to Doctor Johnson at 5 Mesa Street, El Paso, Texas.

_____

8. In September, Mistress Torres's class goes to the animal shelter on River Avenue.

_____

9. Tennessee and Missouri are next to Kentucky.

_____

10. Mistress Brecht spoke at the school on Barstow Road on Friday.

_____

Practice Book
© Harcourt • Grade 3

Name _____

▶ **Read the Spelling Words. Write each word where it belongs.**

Words with *str*

1. _____
2. _____
3. _____
4. _____
5. _____
6. _____
7. _____

Words with *scr*

8. _____
9. _____
10. _____

Words with *spr*

11. _____
12. _____
13. _____
14. _____
15. _____

Spelling Words

1. spray
2. street
3. sprint
4. stripe
5. screen
6. strong
7. spring
8. stray
9. scream
10. strike
11. spread
12. string
13. sprout
14. scratch
15. stream

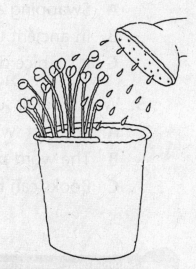

School–Home Connection

Encourage your child to think of other words that begin with these letter patterns and write them down. Then confirm each spelling by looking it up in a dictionary.

69

Name _____

▶ **Read the passage. Then circle the letter of the best answer to each question.**

Did you ever trade one thing for another? It can be fun. It also is a good way to get rid of old things and find yourself some wonderful new treasures. People have been swapping things for thousands of years. In ancient times, money was hard to get. So one family would trade their extra cow for another family's extra pig or horse. Today, people get most of what they need by buying things in stores. But swapping and trading is still going on. You can swap books with a friend. That way, you can trade a book you have read for a book that will be new and exciting to you. You can do the same thing with toys, games, and clothes that no longer fit.

1. What is the main idea of the passage?
   A It's fun!
   B Swapping is a great way to trade old things for new treasures.
   C You can swap books with a friend.

2. Which detail does not support the main idea?

   Tip
   Remember that details help explain the main idea.

   A Swapping and trading is still going on.
   B In ancient times, money was hard to get.
   C It's a nice day.

3. Which detail supports the main idea?
   A You can swap books with a friend.
   B The word *paws* spelled backwards is *swap.*
   C Books can be a great deal of fun.

School–Home Connection
Reread the passage with the student. Then have the student retell the main idea in his or her own words.

70

Name _____

▶ **Make real words by adding *str* or *scr* to the endings in the box. Then write each finished word under the correct heading.**

str		scr

eet	oke	ap	atch	ing	eak	ape	eam

str words   *scr* words

_____   _____

_____   _____

_____   _____

_____   _____

_____   _____

_____

School–Home Connection

Ask the student to blend *str* and *scr* with the ending *-ub*. Have him or her tell you which combination makes a real word and which makes a nonsense word.

71

Name _____

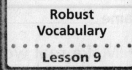

▶ **Choose the correct Vocabulary Word from the box to answer each riddle.**

banquet   agreeable   curiosity
gaze   famine   generous

1. I am quite unusual. You might find me if you hunt through old treasure chests. I am a _____.

2. I can be great fun. I have a lot of delicious food, and you might have to get dressed in fancy clothes. I am a _____.

3. I will not make you sick or unhappy. In fact, you will not find anything wrong with me at all. I am _____.

4. I look at you as though you are the most interesting thing in the world. I _____ at you.

5. I will give you everything I have and more. I am _____.

6. When I am around, people feel very hungry. I am a _____.

▶ **Now it's your turn. Write riddles for the two Vocabulary Words below.**

banquet   generous

7. _____

8. _____

School–Home Connection
Play charades with the student. Take turns giving clues to guess each Vocabulary Word.

72

Practice Book
© Harcourt • Grade 3

Name _____

▶ **As you read "Stone Soup," answer the questions below, and fill in the graphic organizer with the main idea and important details.**

1. What is the main idea of the story? Put it in the Main Idea box.

2. What is one important detail on page 258? Put it in the first Detail box.

3. What is one important detail on page 261? Put it in the second Detail box.

4. What is one important detail on page 271? Put it in the last Detail box.

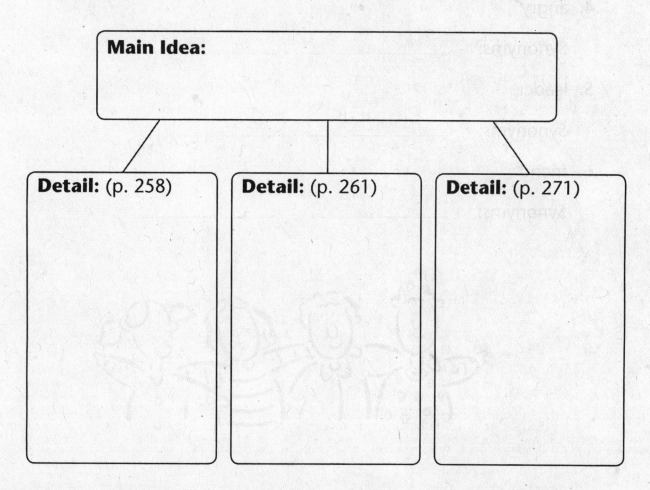

Main Idea:

Detail: (p. 258)

Detail: (p. 261)

Detail: (p. 271)

▶ **Use the information from the graphic organizer above to write a summary of the story on a separate sheet of paper.**

Practice Book
© Harcourt • Grade 3

▶ **Look up each word in a thesaurus. Write two synonyms for the word.**

1. make

   Synonyms: _____ _____

2. walk

   Synonyms: _____ _____

3. sleepy

   Synonyms: _____ _____

4. angry

   Synonyms: _____ _____

5. leader

   Synonyms: _____ _____

6. friend

   Synonyms: _____ _____

Practice Book
© Harcourt • Grade 3

Name _____

▶ Combine letters to make words that have 3 consonants in a row. Start each word with letters from Row 1. End the word with letters from Row 2. The first one has been done for you.

Row 1
st   trans   hun   com   sub   cen   spr   sc   sp   str

Row 2
tral   roller   inkle   tract   ramble   plete   dred   form   read   eam

1. _____stroller_____

2. _____

3. _____

4. _____

5. _____

6. _____

7. _____

8. _____

9. _____

10. _____

School–Home Connection
Ask the student to choose three of these words and use them in sentences.

75

Practice Book
© Harcourt • Grade 3

Name _____

▶ **Write the correct plural form of each singular noun. Use a dictionary if you need to.**

1. pot   _____

2. raspberry   _____

3. tomato   _____

4. meal   _____

5. rabbit   _____

6. moose   _____

7. sheep   _____

8. puppy   _____

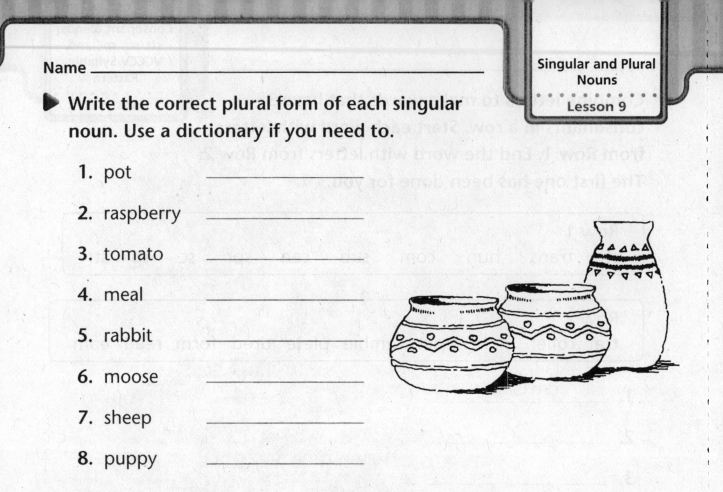

▶ **Rewrite the sentences. Use the plural forms of the nouns in parentheses ( ). Use a dictionary if you need to.**

9. The (child) made (sandwich).

   _____

10. Amber sliced (carrot) and (apple).

   _____

11. Do you want (blueberry) or (peach)?

   _____

12. Brush your (tooth) after you eat the (strawberry).

   _____

Practice Book
© Harcourt • Grade 3

▶ **Write a compound word for each meaning.**
Combine words from the box to make the
compounds.

flower	street	snow	bath	suit
rain	sun	block	light	pot
coat	star	fish	bird	

1. An outside lamp _____

2. A child's winter clothing _____

3. A five-pointed sea creature _____

4. A container for growing plants _____

5. A kind of lotion you put on your skin in the summer

   _____

6. A place where robins go to clean their feathers

   _____

7. A piece of clothing you wear to keep yourself dry

   _____

School–Home Connection

With the student, look around and find three
places or objects whose names are compound
words.

77

▶ **Fold the paper along the dotted line. As each spelling word is read aloud, write it in the blank. Then unfold your paper and check your work. Practice writing any spelling words you missed.**

1. _____

2. _____

3. _____

4. _____

5. _____

6. _____

7. _____

8. _____

9. _____

10. _____

11. _____

12. _____

13. _____

14. _____

15. _____

Spelling Words

1. airplane
2. upstairs
3. something
4. itch
5. chef
6. wheat
7. chance
8. push
9. enjoy
10. moist
11. clown
12. loud
13. sprint
14. street
15. scratch

Name _____

▶ **Read each question. Circle the best answer or answers.**

1. Which two words have the same consonant sound?

   chef   attach   chore

2. Which word has a letter pattern that stands for the /(h)w/ sound?

   want   whether   worry

3. Which word has the /sh/ consonant sound?

   chatter   machine   chair

4. Which word has the same consonant sound as *notch*?

   charge   whirl   shut

5. Which two words have the same consonant sound?

   sheet   chef   cheat

6. Which two words have the /ch/ sound?

   channel   shift   champion

School–Home Connection

Ask the student to identify the consonant
sound that *attach* and *chore* share.

79

Practice Book
© Harcourt • Grade 3

▶ **Read the selection below. Then answer the questions.**

> I love to paint with bright colors. Colors are so interesting! Did you know that just three colors make up almost all the different colors we see? Red, blue, and yellow combine to make many other colors. For example, red and blue make purple. Yellow and red make orange. Yellow and blue make green. And with these colors, a painter can make new colors. Paintings with lots of colors are the most beautiful kind. What kind of paintings do you like?

1. Write two facts from the passage.

_____

_____

_____

2. Write two opinions from the passage.

_____

_____

_____

3. Answer the question in the last sentence of the passage, giving your opinion.

_____

_____

 School–Home Connection

Ask the student to describe a sunset, using both facts and opinions.

80

Name _____

▶ **Write the answer to each question.**

> **Reference Sources**
> dictionary   encyclopedia
> thesaurus   atlas

1. Which reference source would you use to find a synonym

   for *empty*? _____

2. Which reference source would you use to find out which countries

   border Panama? _____

3. Which reference source tells what *lilac* means?

   _____

4. Which reference source describes the climate in which

   palm trees grow and how long it takes them to grow?

   _____

5. Which reference source would you use to find an antonym

   for *pleasant*? _____

 School–Home Connection

Ask the student to name three types of
information found in a dictionary.

88

▶ **Read the selection. Write an answer to each question.**

My class is taking a field trip to a campground next week. I am very excited because we are going to learn how to set up a tent. If the weather is nice, we can even start a fire and roast some marshmallows. We will leave for the trip at 8 A.M. and get to the campsite by 10 A.M. I have a new book to read on the bus. Our teacher will show us how to identify poison ivy and other plants in the woods. The trip will teach us about nature and what it is like to live without many things from the modern world.

1. What is the main idea of the passage?

   _____

   _____

2. What are two supporting details in the passage?

   _____

   _____

   _____

   _____

3. What is a detail that does not support the main idea?

   _____

   _____

School–Home Connection

Ask the student to identify another sentence that tells the main idea of the selection.

87

▶ **Read this part of a student's rough draft.
Then answer the questions that follow.**

> (1) There is a mystery to solve at 10 Mountain <u>Road</u>.
> (2) The Brooks children can't find their puppy. (3) What
> are the clue? (4) The door is open, and cookies are baking
> in the house across the street. (5) _____ Brooks says she
> knows where the puppy is. (6) Do you?

1. What is the abbreviation for
the underlined word in
Sentence 1?
   A rd
   B rd.
   C Rd.
   D RD

2. What is the correct plural form
of the noun in Sentence 3?
   A clue
   B clues
   C cluees
   D cluies

3. How many SINGULAR nouns
are in Sentence 4?
   A two
   B three
   C four
   D five

4. How many PLURAL nouns are
in Sentence 4?
   A one
   B two
   C three
   D four

5. Which abbreviation could go
in the blank in Sentence 5?
   A mrs
   B Mrs
   C MS
   D Mrs.

6. Which sentence has an
irregular plural noun?
   A Sentence 2
   B Sentence 3
   C Sentence 4
   D Sentence 5

Name _____

▶ **Part A. Draw a line from each consonant blend in
Column A to four different letter groups in
Column B to form words.**

Column A   **Column B**

                                                eech

scr   amble

                                                ide

                                                ict

str   ape

                                                ay

                                                uggle

                                                atch

▶ **Part B.**

1. Which letter combination from Column B will make a word with the

   consonant blend *spr*? _____

2. Use this new word in a sentence:

   _____

   _____

   _____

 **School–Home Connection**

Ask the student to think of other letter
combinations that will form a word when
combined with *spr*.

85

Practice Book
© Harcourt • Grade 3

Name _____

▶ **Part A. Complete each sentence with one of the
Vocabulary Words from the Word Box.**

investigate	laboratory	suspect
expert	various	confess

1. Every night, the scientists wash all the beakers in the

_____.

2. When her parents found the flashlight under her pillow, Leigh had

to _____ she had been staying up past her

bedtime to read.

3. I _____ you will not like the reptile

documentary since you are afraid of snakes.

4. Tomorrow, Dad and I will go to the store to

_____.the best kind of food processor to buy.

5. Santino is good at kickball, but he is certainly not an

_____ at the game.

6. This summer, I read _____ books about mice.

▶ **Part B. Write a sentence describing something you might investigate
in a laboratory.**

_____

_____

School–Home Connection
Ask the student to list three things at which he
or she would like to be an expert someday.

84

Practice Book
© Harcourt • Grade 3

Name _____

▶ **Write a synonym or an antonym for the underlined word in each sentence.**

Synonyms

1. It was a dark, <u>chilly</u> night. _____

2. Please <u>throw</u> me the ball. _____

3. We were <u>wet</u> from head to toe. _____

4. What a <u>wonderful</u> time we had! _____

5. Gregg is <u>kind</u> to his Aunt. _____

Antonyms

6. The dog's bowl was <u>empty</u>. _____

7. We took the <u>crooked</u> path. _____

8. I think I made a <u>huge</u> mistake. _____

9. We were all <u>bored</u> by the play. _____

10. He was an <u>excellent</u> teacher. _____

School–Home Connection

Write the sentence: *I feel _____*. Ask the student to fill in the blank with a word that expresses how he or she feels. Then write a synonym and an antonym for that word.

Practice Book
© Harcourt • Grade 3

Name _____

▶ **Read each sentence. Complete each unfinished word by writing *ou*, *ow*, *oi*, or *oy* on the blanks.**

1. I do not like brussels spr_____ _____ts.

2. What time is your doctor's app_____ _____ntment?

3. Try not to ann_____ _____ your little brother.

4. What do you think pigs are saying when they _____ _____nk?

5. The five v_____ _____els are *a, e, i, o,* and *u.*

6. Albert added fl_____ _____r to the bread dough.

7. My mother enj_____ _____s gardening.

8. Be careful not to confuse baking soda with baking p_____ _____der.

School–Home Connection

With the student, come up with four new words, each using one of the above vowel patterns.

Practice Book
© Harcourt • Grade 3

▶ **Read this part of a student's rough draft. Then answer the questions that follow.**

> **(1)** Mrs. Sanchez's class performed a play on _____, October 2. **(2)** The Play was at the Madison Elementary School. **(3)** At 7:00 P.M. **(4)** My sister Elaine acted, she did a great job. **(5)** My bedtime is 8:00 P.M. **(6)** My parents let me stay up late to watch the play.

1. Which word could go in the blank in Sentence 1?
  A Monday
  B tuesday
  C evening
  D lunchtime

2. Which word in Sentence 2 is incorrectly capitalized?
  A Play
  B Madison
  C Elementary
  D School

3. Which word should follow the comma in Sentence 4?
  A but
  B or
  C and
  D tonight

4. Which is the proper noun in Sentence 4?
  A sister
  B Elaine
  C great
  D job

5. Which two simple sentences could be joined by a comma followed by *but*?
  A Sentences 1 and 2
  B Sentences 3 and 4
  C Sentences 4 and 5
  D Sentences 5 and 6

6. Which sentence is NOT complete?
  A Sentence 2
  B Sentence 3
  C Sentence 5
  D Sentence 6

▶ **Read the Spelling Words. Then read the name of each group. Write each word where it belongs.**

Words with *ble*

1. _____

2. _____

3. _____

4. _____

5. _____

Words with *dle*

6. _____   7. _____

Word with *cle*

8. _____

Words with *ple*

9. _____

10. _____

11. _____

Words with *tle*

12. _____   14. _____

13. _____   15. _____

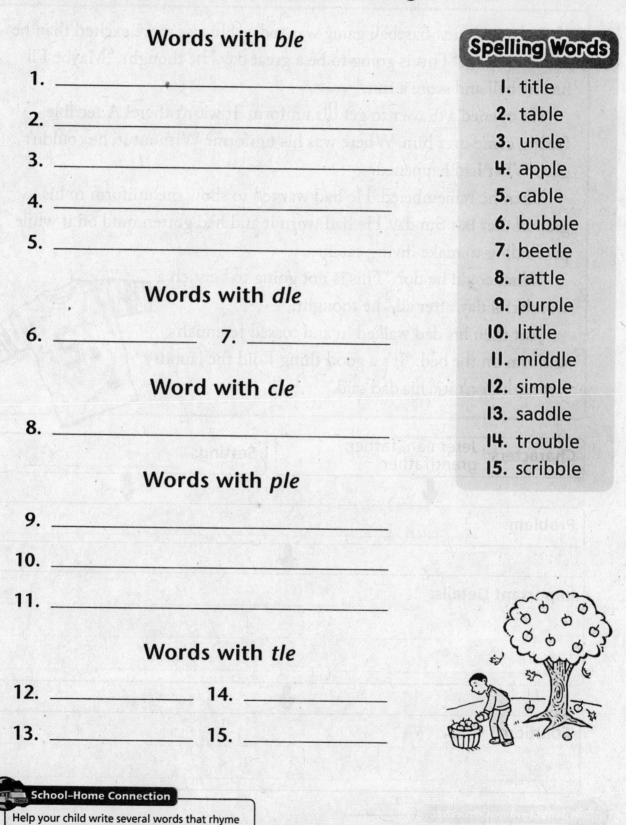

Spelling Words

1. title
2. table
3. uncle
4. apple
5. cable
6. bubble
7. beetle
8. rattle
9. purple
10. little
11. middle
12. simple
13. saddle
14. trouble
15. scribble

School–Home Connection

Help your child write several words that rhyme with *cable, little,* and *bubble.* Discuss the correct spelling of each word. Confirm each word's spelling using a print or an online dictionary.

Practice Book
© Harcourt • Grade 3

▶ **Read the story. Then complete the graphic organizer.**

Jeremiah's first baseball game was today. He was more excited than he had ever been. "This is going to be a great day," he thought. "Maybe I'll hit the ball and score a run."

He opened a drawer to get his uniform. It wasn't there! A terrible feeling came over him. Where was his uniform? Without it, he couldn't play. What had happened?

Then he remembered. He had wanted to show the uniform to his grandfather last Sunday. He had worn it and had gotten mud on it while pretending to make diving catches.

What could he do? "This is not going to be such a wonderful day, after all," he thought.

Just then his dad walked in and tossed Jeremiah's uniform on the bed. "It's a good thing I did the laundry last night, isn't it?" his dad said.

Characters: Jeremiah, father, grandfather

Setting: _____

↓ ↓

Problem: _____

↓

Important Details: _____

_____

_____

↓

Solution: _____

_____

School–Home Connection

Have the student use the graphic organizer as a guide to retell the story to you in his or her own words.

90

Name _____

▶ **Circle the C-*le* word and use it in a sentence.**

1. staple   stapel   stapple

_____

2. muble   mumble   mummble

_____

3. ridel   ridle   riddle

_____

4. starttle   startle   startell

_____

5. padel   paddle   paddoul

_____

6. genttle   genle   gentle

_____

7. cable   cabble   cabel

_____

8. titel   titlle   title

_____

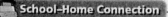
91

Practice Book

© Harcourt • Grade 3

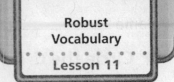

▶ **Read each question. Pay special attention to the Vocabulary Word that is underlined. Then write your answer on the line.**

1. If you <u>sobbed</u> at the end of a movie, how would you describe that movie to a friend?

_____

2. If you hoped to be <u>encouraging</u> to a friend who was about to act in a play, what would you say?

_____

3. When might you hear people <u>chuckling</u>?

_____

4. What is something you could do that would be <u>soothing</u>, especially after working hard?

_____

5. If you had a <u>brief</u> amount of time to eat, what would you eat?

_____

6. When has someone <u>praised</u> you recently?

_____

School–Home Connection

Ask the student to remember something that he or she thinks was soothing. Have the student tell you what *soothing* means.

Practice Book
© Harcourt • Grade 3

▶ As you read "Loved Best," fill in the graphic organizer. Record the important facts you learn along the way.

Section 1 pages 306–308

Characters: Mrs. Lasiter, Carolyn, Mama, Daddy, Granddaddy,

Setting:

Section 2 page 312

Problem:

Section 3 pages 302–319

Important Events:

Section 4 page 320

Solution:

▶ On a separate sheet of paper, summarize the story. Use the graphic organizer to help you.

Practice Book
© Harcourt • Grade 3

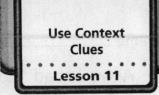

▶ **Read each sentence. Look for a word or words with about the same meaning as the underlined word. Then circle the letter of the best definition for that underlined word.**

1. I grinned at Grandma, and she <u>beamed</u> back at me.

   A smiled

   B growled

   C gave an unhappy look

   D laughed loudly

2. Carolyn's nervous stomach <u>churned</u>, and she thought it would never stop spinning.

   A grew calm

   B turned into butter

   C enjoyed

   D stirred violently

3. The <u>performance</u> was over, and everyone had enjoyed the play.

   A the whole group

   B a happy look

   C show

   D meal

4. The <u>entire</u> class was looking at her, and all of her classmates showed concern.

   A whole

   B wheels of a large truck

   C small

   D best

School-Home Connection

Ask the student to use each underlined word in a sentence.

Practice Book
© Harcourt • Grade 3

Name _____

▶ Write the C-*le* word that goes with each clue.
Then cross out the two syllables in the box that
make up the word you wrote. When you are done,
the leftover syllables will form a word that is "easy"
to read.

bee	gle	bot	ea	crum	ple
ple	dle	fid	tle	dou	ap
ble	cra	sim	tle	dle	ble

1. Another name for a violin _____

2. A place to put a doll or a baby _____

3. To break into many pieces _____

4. A kind of insect _____

5. A container made from glass or plastic _____

6. The national bird of the United States _____

7. A kind of fruit _____

8. Twice as much _____

The word that is "easy" to read is _____

School–Home Connection

Have the student read the words that have
long vowel sounds and tell you the letter or
letters that stand for these sounds.

95

Practice Book
© Harcourt • Grade 3

▶ **Rewrite each phrase. Use the correct possessive noun.**

1. the costumes that belong to the girls

   _____

2. the dance of Ron

   _____

3. the necklace owned by her grandmother

   _____

4. the bottles of the babies

   _____

5. the sleeves of the dresses

   _____

6. the car that belongs to my mother

   _____

▶ **Write sentences using the noun below. The words in parentheses ( ) tell which form of the noun to use.**

dancer

7. (singular) _____

8. (plural) _____

9. (singular possessive) _____

10. (plural possessive) _____

Practice Book
© Harcourt • Grade 3

Name _____

▶ **Make cards for the Spelling Words. Lay them down and read them.**

1. Put the words that have silent letters at the beginning in one group. Then write the words in the chart.

2. Put the words that have silent letters in the middle in one group. Then write the words in the chart.

3. Put the words that have silent letters at the end in another group. Then write the words in the chart.

Spelling Words

1. gnat
2. knew
3. sign
4. knob
5. gnaw
6. write
7. knees
8. wrinkle
9. kneel
10. wrist
11. cough
12. known
13. rough
14. wrench
15. knight

Beginning

1. _____	5. _____	9. _____
2. _____	6. _____	10. _____
3. _____	7. _____	11. _____
4. _____	8. _____	12. _____

Middle	End
13. _____	15. _____
14. _____	16. _____

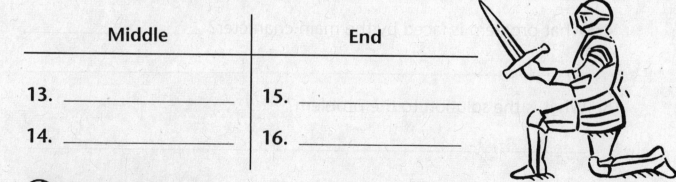

School–Home Connection

Have your child read aloud the list of Spelling Words. Talk about and write other words that have these silent letters.

97

Practice Book
© Harcourt • Grade 3

▶ **Read the story. Then write answers to the questions.**

> Nita was walking the family dog, Abe, when a car raced by. Abe barked. Nita ran home.
>
> "We have to make drivers slow down. These cars could hurt Abe!" Nita said to her father and her older sister.
>
> "Maybe you and your sister can write a letter to the newspaper. The paper will publish it, and a lot of people will read about the cars on our street. That may make some of them drive more slowly," said her father.
>
> "Come on," Nita's sister, Vera, said. "We can do this together."
>
> Nita and Vera wrote the letter. The newspaper sent a reporter to do a story, and Nita and Abe had their picture in the paper! The town put up a sign on Nita's street. It read, "Please slow down. Children and pets live here. Drive slowly!" People now drive slowly down Nita's street.

1. Who is the main character?

   _____

2. Who are the other characters? _____

   _____

3. What is a very important event in the story?

   _____

4. What problem is faced by the main character? _____

   _____

5. What is the solution to the problem?

   _____

   _____

Practice Book
© Harcourt • Grade 3

▶ **Unscramble the underlined letters and write the word on the line.**

1. A small creature that appears in old stories is a meong.

   _____

2. Tapping on a door or a window is called gcoinnkk.

   _____

3. Very small insects that sometimes swarm around people are stang.

   _____

4. A brave soldier from the Middle Ages is a kingth.

   _____

5. You can make tnsok with string or rope.

   _____

6. Gary slowly turned the round nbok on the door.

   _____

7. The hungry cougar edgnwa on a tender bone.

   _____

8. Sharon's keens were very strong because she walked uphill every day.

   _____

9. The stop nigs was bright red.

   _____

10. Please lenke at the water's edge, and quietly watch the manatees swim.

    _____

Practice Book
© Harcourt • Grade 3

Name _____

▶ **Pick the word from the Word Box that best fits with each group of three words. Write the word on the line.**

translate	bothersome	dodging
din	heaving	repairs

1. loud
crowded
yelling

_____

2. annoying
pesky
disturb

_____

3. fix
patch
mend

_____

4. words
change
language

_____

5. escaping
quick
diving

_____

6. earth
moving
quaking

_____

School–Home Connection

Have the student show you a **dodging** movement. Then have him or her imitate how a **bothersome** person might act.

Practice Book
© Harcourt • Grade 3

▶ As you read "A Pen Pal for Max," fill in the graphic organizer with important information from the story.

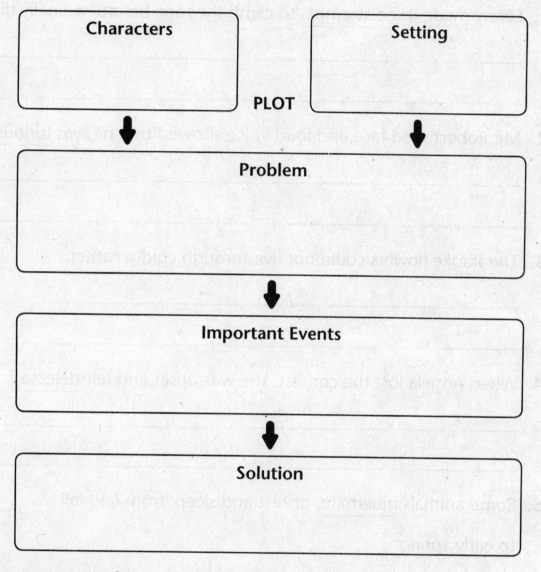

Characters

Setting

PLOT

Problem

Important Events

Solution

▶ On a separate sheet of paper, summarize the selection. Use the graphic organizer to help you.

Name _____

▶ **Write a definition for each underlined word.**
Next to the definition, describe the context
clues that helped you understand what the word means.

1. Lenny made three <u>attempts</u> to climb the rope before he finally did it.

_____

_____

2. Mr. Robert's red face and loud voice showed that he was <u>furious</u>.

_____

_____

3. The <u>fragile</u> flowers could not live through cold weather.

_____

_____

4. When Angela lost the contest, she was upset and felt <u>dejected</u>.

_____

_____

5. Some animals <u>hibernate</u>, or rest and sleep, from late fall

to early spring.

_____

_____

▶ **Read the sentence. Circle the correct spelling**
for the missing word. Then write the word
on the line.

1. I _____ on the door, but no one answered.

    knocked   gnocked   nocked

2. Sam likes to _____ with his brother.

    restle   westle   wrestle

3. I set the table with a _____ and a fork.

    nife   gnife   knife

4. When I hear a funny joke, I _____.

    laugh   laff   lafe

5. Does the _____ on that house say "For Sale"?

    sien   sign   sikn

6. Mr. Wright has lots of interesting _____ in his attic.

    stuff   staugh   stough

7. The answer he gave me was _____.

    rong   grong   wrong

8. I have a sore spot on my _____.

    gneck   neck   kneck

Name _____

▶ **Write the pronoun in each sentence.**
Then label each as S (singular) or P (plural).

1. We learned about Chile today. _____

2. Mr. Edwards showed us two maps. _____

3. He hung the maps on the wall. _____

4. They showed volcanoes and a desert. _____

5. The students looked at them carefully. _____

6. Mr. Edwards asked me to point to the desert. _____

▶ **Rewrite each sentence with a correct pronoun.**

7. Ellen studied Spanish because _____ wanted to visit Spain.

_____

8. The class was fun, and the students enjoyed _____.

_____

9. The teacher brought pictures to show _____.

_____

10. He took the pictures when _____ was in Spain.

_____

104

▶ **Read the Spelling Words. Sort the words and write them where they belong.**

Words with /s/ Sound Spelled with c

1. _____

2. _____

3. _____

4. _____

5. _____

6. _____

Words with /j/ Sound Spelled with g, or dge

7. _____

8. _____

9. _____

10. _____

11. _____

12. _____

13. _____

14. _____

15. _____

Spelling Words

1. ice
2. age
3. rice
4. edge
5. stage
6. giant
7. range
8. judge
9. ledge
10. police
11. recent
12. bridge
13. office
14. strange
15. central

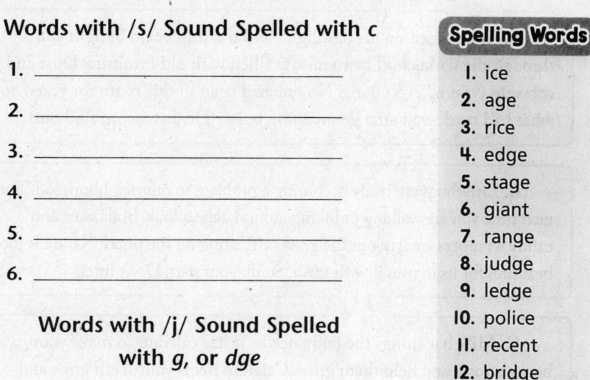

School–Home Connection

Help your child write a list of words that have the soft c or g sound. Discuss the correct spelling for each word. Together, confirm each spelling using a print or an online dictionary.

Practice Book
© Harcourt • Grade 3

Name _____

▶ **Read each paragraph. Then write the answers to the questions.**

> **A.** Sam turned on his flashlight, and the thin beam of light cut through the darkness. The room was filled with old furniture. Dust and cobwebs covered everything. No one had been in this room for years. So what had made that strange moaning noise? He just *had* to find out!

> **B.** Litterbugs are really becoming a problem in our neighborhood. The next time you are walking or biking around, take a look. Soda cans and candy wrappers are lying in the grass or floating on the pond. Nature is too beautiful for us to ruin it with trash. So do your part. Don't litter!

> **C.** Milk has things the body needs. It has calcium to make your bones strong and help them grow. Calcium helps your teeth grow and stay healthy, too. Milk has lots of protein to build strong muscles.

1. What is the author's purpose in paragraph A? Who is the main character? _____

   _____

2. What is the author's purpose in paragraph B? Why do you think so?

   _____

   _____

3. What is the author's purpose in paragraph C? Why do you think so?

   _____

   _____

School–Home Connection

Have the student write three sentences to persuade you to do an activity with him or her. Remind the student to support the main idea with detail in the sentences.

106

▶ **Read the story. Complete the spelling of each word. Use -ge or -dge.**

Last month, I was in a play called "The Lar_____ Bird."

The play takes place in a town called Bri_____ View. In the

story, a stran_____ oran_____ bird flies into town and

sits on a le_____ at the top of the town hall. The people of

the town try to capture the bird and put it in a ca_____.

But they cannot quite reach the e_____ of the roof where

the bird is sitting!

I played a girl who is eight years of a_____. She tells the

people that the bird is never going to bu_____ and that

they should just leave the bird alone. The people of the

town chan_____ their minds. They decide to let the bird

stay on top of the building. It is a great play!

School–Home Connection

Have the student tell a new story that uses several -ge and -dge words.

Practice Book
© Harcourt • Grade 3

Name _____

▶ **Part A. Read each group of words. Write the Vocabulary Word that belongs in the group.**

> dissolve   absorb   protects
> rustling   columns   particles

1. shields   guards   saves   _____

2. crackling   shuffling   crunching   _____

3. melt   disappear   mix   _____

4. take in   soak up   sop up   _____

▶ **Part B. Complete the sentences.**

5. The **columns** of a library might be made out of _____

_____

6. If you find **particles** of glass on your kitchen floor, someone probably

_____

7. To **protect** your CD collection, you should _____

_____

8. Something that **dissolves** quickly in water is _____

_____

School-Home Connection

With the student, discuss a building you have
seen that has columns. Come up with a list of
adjectives to describe the columns.

108

Practice Book
© Harcourt • Grade 3

▶ As you read "A Tree Is Growing," fill the graphic organizer.

Section 1 pages 372–379

What I Know:	What I Read:	Author's Purpose

Section 2 pages 380–387

What I Know:	What I Read:	Author's Purpose

Section 3 pages 388–393

What I Know:	What I Read:	Author's Purpose

1. What do you already know about trees?

_____

2. What is the first thing you read about trees?

_____

▶ On a separate sheet of paper, summarize what you learned about trees. Use the graphic organizer to help you.

Name _____

▶ **Use the graphic aid to answer the questions.**
Circle the letter of the best answer to each question.

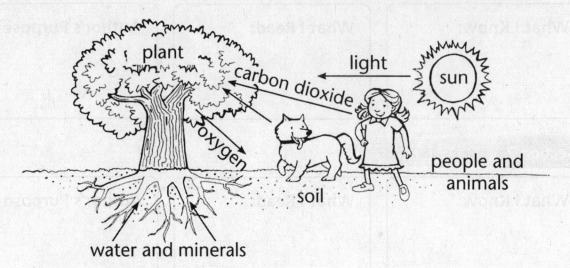

1. What does the sun bring to the plant?

   A carbon dioxide

   B oxygen

   C water and minerals

   D light

2. What do people and animals bring to the plant?

   A carbon dioxide

   B oxygen

   C water and minerals

   D soil

3. What does the plant bring to people and animals?

   A carbon dioxide

   B oxygen

   C water and minerals

   D sun

School–Home Connection

Work with the student to create a graphic
aid illustrating a system or process such as a
weather pattern or how a flower grows.

Practice Book
© Harcourt • Grade 3

Name _____

Words with
Consonants /s/c
and /j/g dge
Lesson 13

▶ Each line of letters has two hidden words in which c is pronounced with the s sound or g is pronounced with the j sound. Circle the hidden words. Then write a sentence of your own that has both hidden words.

1. c e j u o r a n f o r c e b l g e s p g i a n t c e c i o l

_____

_____

2. a c i f c e g i p p e n c i l g e r y g e r m s c e r w o t

_____

_____

3. g j u d g e f g e n t l e v c e h t c i z t c i e g i d g

_____

_____

4. o s k e r g e c i c d a n c e o l g i c e o l i m s t a g e

_____

_____

5. g e a r c e i d g e c i e d g e p r i n c e t r a i p g i c

_____

_____

Practice Book
© Harcourt • Grade 3

▶ **Write a subject or object pronoun to replace each underlined word or phrase.**

1. <u>Ariel's sister</u> taught <u>Ariel</u> about bees. _____

2. <u>Ariel's sister</u> told <u>Ariel</u> that bees are insects. _____

3. <u>Ariel and I</u> watched bees in the park. _____

4. Ariel and I saw <u>the bees</u> fly. _____

5. Ariel's father gave <u>Ariel and me</u> a book. _____

6. <u>The book</u> had pictures of bees. _____

▶ **Rewrite each sentence. Use *I* and *me* correctly.**

7. You and me picked pears from the tree.

   _____

8. Todd ate cherries with my friend and I.

   _____

9. Me and my brother sliced apples.

   _____

10. They shared the plums with me and him.

   _____

School–Home Connection

Have your child write sentences using one or
more of the following pronouns:
I you he she him her we they us

Practice Book
© Harcourt • Grade 3

► Read the Spelling Words. Sort the words and
write them where they belong.

Words that end with *n*

1. _____

2. _____

3. _____

4. _____

5. _____

6. _____

7. _____

Words that end with *l*

8. _____

9. _____

10. _____

11. _____

12. _____

► Put the words that are left in alphabetical order.

13. _____

14. _____

15. _____

Spelling Words

1. robin
2. petal
3. seven
4. solid
5. final
6. given
7. color
8. hotel
9. wagon
10. music
11. total
12. cabin
13. taken
14. pupil
15. broken

School–Home Connection

As you and your child discuss your daily
activities, write down words that have the same
syllable patterns as *robin* and *hotel*. Go over the
list and have your child say and spell each word.

Practice Book
© Harcourt • Grade 3

► **Read the selection. Then answer the questions that follow.**

Leave the Logs Alone

Have you ever walked through a forest? If so, you probably have seen logs on the forest floor. Some people think these fallen trees are no longer useful. They think the logs should be removed to clean up the forest. But that's not true. Fallen trees still have a purpose.

Animals use these logs for shelter and to find food. If you gently rolled a log and peeked underneath, you would be surprised at what you would find. Worms, grubs, insects, and snakes make their homes in the cool mud beneath the logs. Removing the logs would mean that all of these creatures would have to find new homes.

In time, the logs will rot and become soil. New plants and trees will grow in that soil. This is another reason that fallen trees are important.

As you can see, it is helpful to the forest to leave fallen trees where they are. We should leave the logs alone.

1. What was the author's purpose for writing this selection?

   _____

   _____

2. How does the title help you know this?

   _____

   _____

3. What other sentences give you clues about the author's purpose?

   _____

   _____

   _____

School-Home Connection
Have the student share a story with you. Work together to determine the author's purpose.

▶ **Look at each pair of spelling words. Choose the word in each pair that has the V/CV syllable pattern, and write it on the lines. Use the boxed letters to answer the riddle at the bottom of the page.**

1. vanish   broken   ☐ ____ ____ ____ ____ ____

2. total   wagon   ☐ ____

3. taken   seven   ____ ☐ ____ ____ ____

4. cabin   music   ____ ☐ ____ ____

5. final   given   ____ ____ ____ ____ ____

6. robin   pupil   ____ ☐ ____ ____ ____

7. hotel   color   ____ ____ ☐ ____ ____

Riddle:

Where can you leave your dog when you go to the mall?

Answer:

In the

____ ____ __R__ ____ ____ __G__ ____ __O__ ____.
  1   2   3   4   5   6   7

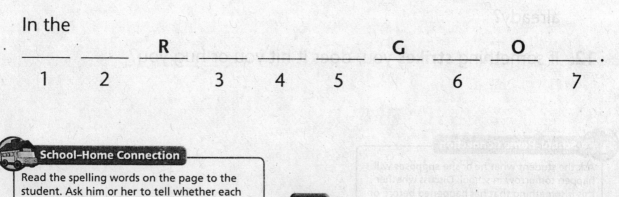

School–Home Connection

Read the spelling words on the page to the student. Ask him or her to tell whether each word has a long or short vowel sound.

115

Practice Book
© Harcourt • Grade 3

Name _____

▶ **Part A.** Write the Vocabulary Word from the
Word Box that matches each idea.

┌─────────────────────────────────────┐
│   maze   glimpse   spears   │
│   suppose   strikes   roost   │
└─────────────────────────────────────┘

1. _____ when you think something may happen

2. _____ a winding path that is like a puzzle

3. _____ what a bird does to settle in a tree's branches

4. _____ a quick peek at something

5. _____ when something hits someone

6. _____ to stick a sharp object through something

▶ **Part B.** Use what you know about the Vocabulary Words in dark type
to answer each question. Circle the answer within the sentence.

7. If you get a **glimpse** of a frog, do you get a long look or a quick look?

8. If someone **spears** a piece of fruit, does he use a fork or a spoon?

9. If a bird **roosts**, is it flying or resting?

10. If you are in a **maze**, are you on a straight path or a winding path?

11. If you **suppose** something, might it happen or did it happen

    already?

12. If something **strikes** you, does it hit you or hug you?

School–Home Connection

Ask the student what he or she **supposes** will
happen tomorrow in school. Discuss whether
this is something that has happened before or
if it is something completely new.

116

▶ As you read "One Small Place in a Tree," fill in the first column of the graphic organizer with what you already know. In the middle column, write the information you read. Fill in the author's purpose after you finish the selection.

What I Know	What I Read	Author's Purpose

1. What is the main reason the author wrote the selection?

_____

_____

2. What is the author's purpose?

_____

_____

▶ On a separate sheet of paper, summarize the selection. Use the graphic organizer to help you.

Name _____

▶ The following graph shows the kinds of trees in Sunshine Park. Use the information in the graph to answer the questions. Answer each question with a complete sentence.

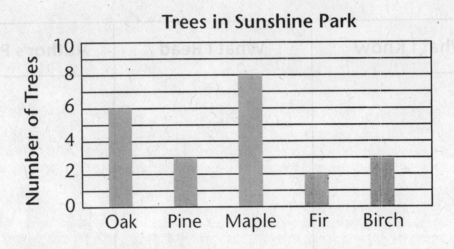

Trees in Sunshine Park

1. What kinds of trees does Sunshine Park have?

_____

2. How many maple trees are there in the park?

_____

3. What kind of tree has the fewest number in the park?

_____

4. How many pine trees are there in the park?

_____

5. The park has an equal number of which two kinds of trees?

_____

School–Home Connection

Work with the student to create a new graph using the following information: ash trees, 10; cherry trees, 7; willow trees, 2.

118

▶ **Use these VCV words to complete each sentence.
Then circle those words in the puzzle. Look for
them across and down.**

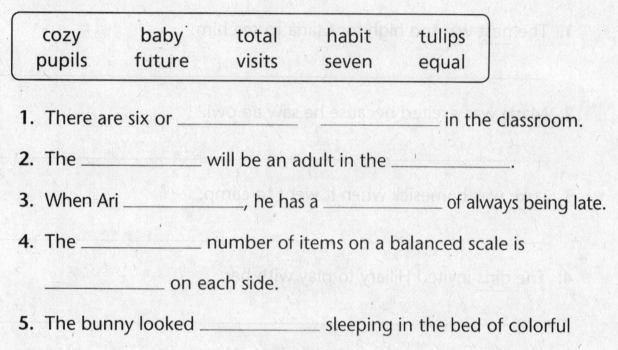

cozy	baby	total	habit	tulips
pupils	future	visits	seven	equal

1. There are six or _____ _____ in the classroom.

2. The _____ will be an adult in the _____.

3. When Ari _____, he has a _____ of always being late.

4. The _____ number of items on a balanced scale is

   _____ on each side.

5. The bunny looked _____ sleeping in the bed of colorful

   _____.

T	Y	R	Q	B	C	E	T	D	S
R	F	I	L	A	Y	E	O	I	E
A	U	T	D	B	N	Q	T	N	V
W	T	F	A	Y	N	U	A	A	E
L	U	U	G	L	E	A	L	T	N
R	R	B	T	H	N	L	N	U	T
N	E	P	U	P	I	L	S	L	S
W	C	O	Z	Y	P	Y	N	I	Q
H	A	B	I	T	Z	N	T	P	O
V	I	S	I	T	S	L	S	S	M

School–Home Connection

Ask the student to tell where each VCV word
is divided into syllables. Then have him or her
suggest other VCV words that could be used to
complete the sentences.

119

Name _____

▶ **Circle the pronoun in each sentence. Rewrite the sentence. Correct the pronoun so that it agrees with the underlined word.**

1. The <u>nest</u> was too high for Maria to see him.

   _____

2. <u>Maria</u> was excited because he saw an owl.

   _____

3. <u>Luke</u> was homesick when it went to camp.

   _____

4. The <u>girls</u> invited Hillary to play with her.

   _____

5. John wrote a <u>letter</u> and sent them home.

   _____

6. <u>John's</u> parents wrote back to it.

   _____

▶ **Fill in each blank with a correct pronoun. Then underline the word or words that the pronoun refers to.**

7. Honeybees live in hives, where _____ have jobs to do.

8. Worker bees feed the queen bee and protect _____.

9. Honeybees gather nectar and use _____ to make honey.

10. Some people keep bees and collect honey from _____.

School–Home Connection

Ask your child to write three sentences about family members, using their names. Then ask him or her to rewrite the sentences, replacing the names with pronouns.

120

Name _____

▶ **Read the -*le* words in the Word Box. Write each word on a line below. Then divide each word into syllables.**

table	cable	title
maple	noble	staple

C-*le* Words

_____

_____

_____

_____

_____

_____

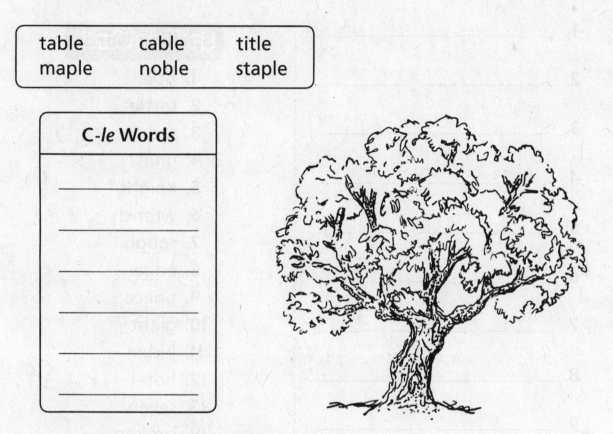

Write two more C-*le* syllable pattern words.

_____

_____

Choose a C-*le* word from the Word Box. Write a sentence using that word.

_____

_____

School–Home Connection

Have the student think of other -*le* words.
Discuss how to divide the new words into
syllables.

121

Practice Book
© Harcourt • Grade 3

Name _____

▶ Fold the paper along the dotted line. As each spelling word is read aloud, write it on the line. Then unfold the paper and check your work.

1. _____

2. _____

3. _____

4. _____

5. _____

6. _____

7. _____

8. _____

9. _____

10. _____

11. _____

12. _____

13. _____

14. _____

15. _____

Spelling Words

1. title
2. rattle
3. saddle
4. gnat
5. knight
6. wrench
7. rough
8. edge
9. police
10. giant
11. judge
12. hotel
13. seven
14. broken
15. taken

School–Home Connection

Ask the student to write five sentences using his or her favorite spelling words from the list above.

122

▶ **Circle the words in each sentence that contain *kn, gn, wr,* or *gh*. Then, write the words in the crossword puzzle.**

1. There is a wrinkle in my new shirt.

2. I tapped on the door with my knuckles.

3. The knight rode a white horse.

4. We knew all the answers on the spelling test.

5. She put wrapping paper on the gift for her friend.

6. He had a bad cough while he was sick.

7. Can you hear the laughter on the playground?

8. Turn left at the stop sign.

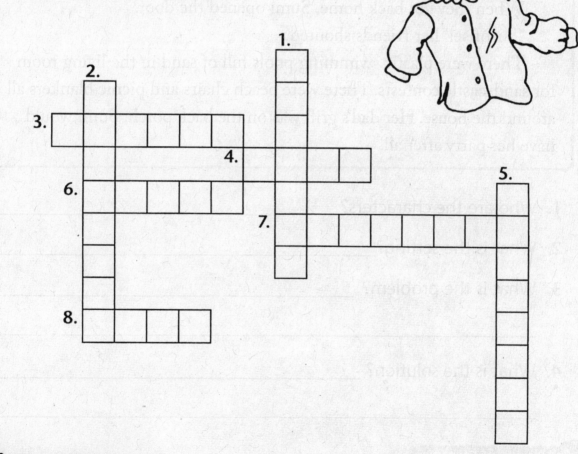

School–Home Connection

Ask the student to think of other words that contain *kn, gn, wr,* and *gh*. Help him or her add several of these words to the puzzle.

123

Practice Book
© Harcourt • Grade 3

Name _____

▶ **Read the story. Then answer the questions.**

Sumi could not believe that today had finally arrived! She had waited all summer for her birthday. She and her mom had planned for weeks. They called it "The Big Beach Birthday Bash." She had invited all her friends for games, swimming, and a cookout at the beach.

Sumi's excitement quickly ended when she looked out the window. Dark storm clouds filled the sky. Within minutes, lightning cracked and rain poured down. She had never been so disappointed.

"We'll figure something out," her mom assured her.

Meanwhile, Sumi's dad took her to the grocery store to pick up meat for the burgers and ice for the cooler.

"Why are we buying this?" she asked. "We can't go to the beach in the rain."

When they got back home, Sumi opened the door.

"Surprise!" her friends shouted.

There were plastic swimming pools full of sand in the living room for sand-castle contests. There were beach chairs and picnic blankets all around the house. Her dad's grill was on the back porch. Sumi would have her party after all!

1. Who are the characters? _____

2. What is the setting? _____

3. What is the problem? _____

_____

4. What is the solution? _____

_____

▶ **Read this part of a student's rough draft.
Then answer the questions that follow.**

> (1) Tony is the friend of Joan. (2) Tony tells Joan that he is upset. (3) Joan asks he what is wrong. (4) Tony says that he lost his mothers pen. (5) Joan helps him look for the pen. (6) Together they find it under Tony's bed.

1. Which sentence has a singular possessive noun?

 A Sentence 2

 B Sentence 3

 C Sentence 5

 D Sentence 6

2. Which sentence has an incorrectly written possessive noun?

 A Sentence 2

 B Sentence 3

 C Sentence 4

 D Sentence 6

3. Which phrase could replace the underlined phrase in Sentence 1?

 A the friend's of Joan

 B the friends of Joan

 C Joan's friend

 D Joans' friend

4. Which pronoun could replace the underlined word in Sentence 2?

 A he

 B she

 C him

 D her

5. Which pronoun could replace the underlined phrase in Sentence 5?

 A it

 B her

 C him

 D them

6. Which sentence has an incorrect pronoun?

 A Sentence 3

 B Sentence 4

 C Sentence 5

 D Sentence 6

Name _____

▶ Follow the path from the arrow to the finish line. Shade only the boxes that have a word with the soft *c* or soft *g* sound. Then answer the questions.

Start	stage	forget	coat	uncover	popcorn	gum
guppy	edge	celery	castle	mice	margin	trace
stag	game	engine	pack	prince	tic	Finish
cast	green	cell	voice	judge	gave	leg

1. Which words in the puzzle end with *-dge*? _____

2. Which words end with the letters *-ice*? _____

3. Which word ends with the letters *-ace*? _____

4. Write three words from above that have the soft *c* sound.

_____

5. Write three words from above that have the soft *g* sound.

_____

126

Name _____

▶ **Part A. Write the meaning of each word in dark type. Underline the clues that helped you figure out the meaning of that word.**

1. Mom asked me to put the forks in the drawer with the other **utensils.**

   Utensils means _____

2. Mario's new glasses **magnify** things, making them bigger and easier

   for him to see.

   Magnify means _____

3. The President is elected by the **citizens** that live in our country.

   Citizens means _____

4. All the noise and confusion was quite a **commotion.**

   Commotion means _____

5. The collector said it was hard to find **obscure** artwork that not

   many people knew about.

   Obscure means _____

▶ **Part B. Fill in the blanks, using some words in dark type from above.**

6. We set the table with plates, cups, and _____.

7. Patti had to _____ the tiny print to be able to see it.

8. All of the _____ at the playground made it hard to

   sit and read.

School–Home Connection

With the student, look for other unfamiliar
words and use context clues to determine
their meaning.

127

▶ **Part A.** Use the meaning of the underlined
Vocabulary Word to complete each sentence.

1. I would need to ask for <u>advice</u> if _____

   _____

2. If a friend asked me to <u>recommend</u> something fun to do on a rainy

   day, I would suggest _____ because

   _____

3. It would not be <u>sensible</u> to _____

   _____

4. I always <u>consult</u> _____ when

   _____

▶ **Part B.** Write a sentence for the Vocabulary Words *issue* and *devise*.

   _____

   _____

   _____

   _____

School–Home Connection

With the student, think of a time when you
have offered advice. Discuss the situation,
challenging the student to use as many of the
Vocabulary Words as possible.

128

Name _____

▶ There are five V/CV words and five VC/V words in the puzzle. The V/CV words are written across. The VC/V words are written down. Circle the words in the puzzle. Then write each one in the correct box at the bottom of the page.

a	t	i	g	e	r	k	s
r	b	a	c	o	r	n	o
i	t	o	t	a	l	v	l
v	w	h	r	s	t	e	i
e	a	a	e	q	l	r	d
r	g	b	n	y	p	y	t
a	o	i	p	u	p	i	l
z	n	t	m	e	v	e	n

V/CV

VC/V

School–Home Connection

Have the student think of three other V/CV and three other VC/V words. Then work together to make a word-search puzzle that includes these words.

Practice Book
© Harcourt • Grade 3

► **Read this part of a student's rough draft.
Then answer the questions that follow.**

(1) Yasmin writes for a newspaper that she started. (2) She reports on what is new in school. (3) Yesterday Yasmin wrote about something that happened to her. (4) She found a kitten in the school playground. (5) Yasmin took the kitten home and gave them to her father. (6) Her father was happy to have the kitten.

1. Which word does the pronoun in Sentence 1 refer to?
   A Yasmin
   B writes
   C newspaper
   D she

2. Which sentence has a singular subject pronoun?
   A Sentence 2
   B Sentence 3
   C Sentence 5
   D Sentence 6

3. Which sentence has a singular object pronoun?
   A Sentence 2
   B Sentence 3
   C Sentence 4
   D Sentence 6

4. Which sentence has a pronoun that does not agree with the noun that it refers to?
   A Sentence 1
   B Sentence 2
   C Sentence 3
   D Sentence 5

5. Which could replace the underlined words in Sentence 6?
   A a singular subject pronoun
   B a plural subject pronoun
   C a singular object pronoun
   D a plural object pronoun

6. Which pronoun could replace the words *the kitten* in Sentence 5?
   A she
   B it
   C they
   D them

▶ **Read the article. On the lines below it, write your answers to the questions about the author's purpose.**

My name is William Wu. I would like to be your Student Council president. I think I would make a good president. I am a responsible student, with exciting ideas for improving our school.

First, I would work with the school to change the school lunch menu. I think it should include some healthy choices. It should also have some foods everyone likes.

Next, I would like our school to have a carnival every year. We could use some of the money we make to buy a new computer for the library. This would help all of our students. We could give the rest of the money to a good cause. This would help our community.

If you like these ideas, vote for me for Student Council president.

1. What was the author's purpose for writing the article?

_____

2. What clues helped you figure out the author's purpose?

_____

_____

3. What does William want readers to know?

_____

_____

_____

School–Home Connection

With the student, create a story. Decide on the author's purpose. Will it be to entertain, to inform, or to persuade?

Practice Book
© Harcourt • Grade 3

Name _____

▶ **Use the information in the diagram to answer the questions.**

Diagram of a Friendly Letter

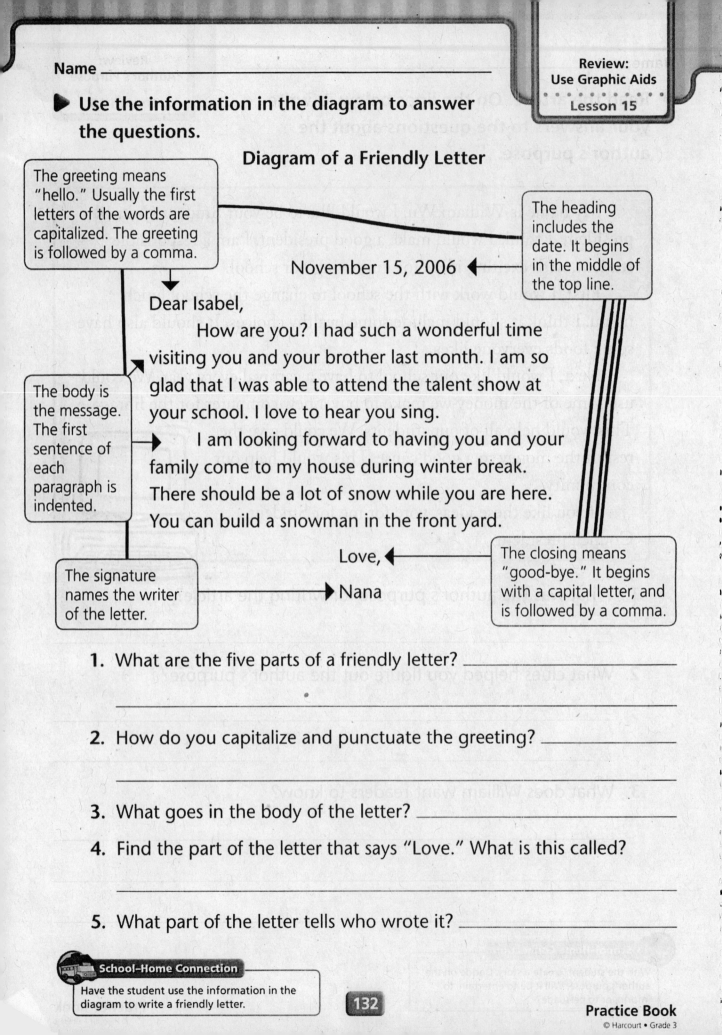

The greeting means "hello." Usually the first letters of the words are capitalized. The greeting is followed by a comma.

The heading includes the date. It begins in the middle of the top line.

November 15, 2006

Dear Isabel,

How are you? I had such a wonderful time visiting you and your brother last month. I am so glad that I was able to attend the talent show at your school. I love to hear you sing.

I am looking forward to having you and your family come to my house during winter break. There should be a lot of snow while you are here. You can build a snowman in the front yard.

The body is the message. The first sentence of each paragraph is indented.

Love,

Nana

The signature names the writer of the letter.

The closing means "good-bye." It begins with a capital letter, and is followed by a comma.

1. What are the five parts of a friendly letter? _____

_____

2. How do you capitalize and punctuate the greeting? _____

_____

3. What goes in the body of the letter? _____

4. Find the part of the letter that says "Love." What is this called?

_____

5. What part of the letter tells who wrote it? _____

School–Home Connection

Have the student use the information in the diagram to write a friendly letter.

Practice Book
© Harcourt • Grade 3

r-Controlled
Vowels /ôr/ or,
ore, our, oar, ar
Lesson 16

Name _____

▶ **Sort and write the Spelling Words with *ar*, *ore*,
oar, *our*, and *or*.**

Words with *ar*

1. _____

2. _____

3. _____

Words with *ore* and *oar*

4. _____

5. _____

6. _____

7. _____

8. _____

Words with *or* and *our*

9. _____

10. _____

11. _____

12. _____

13. _____

14. _____

15. _____

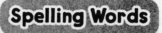

Spelling Words

1. coarse
2. warm
3. soar
4. wore
5. swarm
6. form
7. story
8. warn
9. bore
10. sport
11. glory
12. force
13. course
14. before
15. fourth

School–Home Connection

With your child write a short poem that
includes words with *r*-Controlled vowels such
as those above. Give your poem to family
members to read.

Practice Book
© Harcourt • Grade 3

▶ **Read the story. Then answer the questions below.**

Two mice lived on a farm. One was named Meany, and the other was named Silly. One day the farmer's wife set a big piece of cheese on the kitchen table. Both mice looked at it, and their stomachs rumbled. "I know how we can get the cheese," said Meany. "I will scare the farmer's wife so that she bumps into the table and knocks the cheese to the floor. Then *you* will scare her so that she runs out the door."

Silly shook his head. "I know a better way," he said. Silly ran into the kitchen and did a funny dance. The farmer's wife laughed and laughed. She liked Silly's dance so much that she gave him a big hunk of cheese. To Meany, she gave nothing, and his stomach is still rumbling to this very day.

1. Who are the two main characters?

_____

2. What do they want to do?

_____

3. How are the characters alike?

_____

_____

4. How are the characters different?

_____

_____

_____

School–Home Connection

Help the student compare and contrast two characters in a story he or she enjoys. Ask the student to tell how the characters are alike and how they are different.

Practice Book
© Harcourt • Grade 3

▶ **Circle the word that matches each description.
Then underline the letters that stand for the
/ôr/ sound in that word.**

1. What you call clothes that you had on yesterday

   warm   worn   worse

2. A contest or a game

   spring   sport   splash

3. The opposite of *after*

   fort   because   before

4. The energy to move something

   force   fourth   farce

5. Something you write, tell, or read

   story   sorry   stare

Try This

On a separate sheet of paper, use the words you circled to make new
sentences. Read your sentences aloud to a partner.

School–Home Connection
Have the student tell a story using the circled
words from above.

135

Practice Book
© Harcourt • Grade 3

▶ **Part A**

Write the Vocabulary Word from the box below that completes each sentence.

disguised	cunning	embraced
tender	brittle	delighted

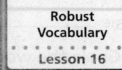

1. When you use a costume to hide who you are, you are _____.

2. If something is _____, it may break apart if you squeeze it.

3. A _____ person can play a clever trick on you.

4. If you can cut something easily, it is probably _____.

5. When people win a prize, they feel _____.

6. Ruth _____ her grandmother when she arrived for a visit.

▶ **Part B**

Write a sentence to answer each question.

7. What could a child do to delight his or her mother?

_____

_____

8. How would you know if a friend was disguised?

_____

_____

School–Home Connection

Help the student name synonyms for the
following Vocabulary Words: *tender, delighted,*
and *cunning.* Then have him or her choose one
word and use it in a written sentence.

136

► As you read "Lon Po Po," fill in the
graphic organizer with details about
how the characters are alike and different.
Then answer the questions.

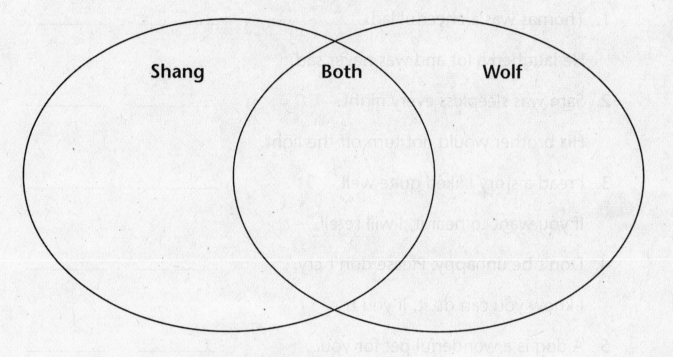

Shang   Both   Wolf

1. How is Shang different from the wolf?

_____

2. How are Shang and the wolf alike?

_____

► On a separate sheet of paper, summarize the selection. Use the
graphic organizer to help you.

Practice Book
© Harcourt • Grade 3

Name _____

▶ **For each rhyme, underline the word with the
prefix or suffix. Then write the prefix or suffix
in the correct column.**

	Prefix	**Suffix**

1. Thomas was a cheerful lad.

   He laughed a lot and was never sad. _____ _____

2. Sam was sleepless every night.

   His brother would not turn off the light. _____ _____

3. I read a story I liked quite well.

   If you want to hear it, I will retell. _____ _____

4. Don't be unhappy. Please don't cry. _____ _____

   I know you can do it, if you try.

5. A dog is a wonderful pet for you. _____ _____

   Cats and birds make nice friends, too.

6. Shonda was careful when riding her bike. _____ _____

   She did not want to hit her buddy, Mike.

Practice Book
© Harcourt • Grade 3

Name _____

r-Controlled
Vowels: *or, ore,
our, ar, oar*

Lesson 16

Read the story. Find ten words with the /ôr/ sound spelled *or, ore, our, ar,* or *oar*. Underline them. Then write the word and the letters that stand for the /ôr/ sound on the lines below.

> Will was on vacation with his family. It was their first day in Florida. Will was so excited that he jumped out of bed. He couldn't wait to see the Atlantic Ocean. But then he heard his sister, Cora, say, "It's pouring outside! Look, Will!"
>
> "We won't be visiting the seashore today," he told her. "It looks like you can put away that surfboard."
>
> "Of course, I warned you," said Cora. "The weather forecast said it would be stormy today. But you didn't listen to me."
>
> Then the cordless telephone rang. It was their cousin, Jorge. He invited Will and Cora to his home to play card games!

1. _____

2. _____

3. _____

4. _____

5. _____

6. _____

7. _____

8. _____

9. _____

10. _____

School–Home Connection

Help the student write two more sentences to continue the story. Help him or her include two new *r*-controlled vowel words.

139

Practice Book
© Harcourt • Grade 3

▶ **Underline the two adjectives in each sentence. Then write whether each adjective tells *what kind* or *how many*.**

1. Many wolves eat five pounds of food a day.

   _____

2. A few wolves have blue eyes.

   _____

3. The coats of some wolves are white.

   _____

4. Big wolves weigh more than ninety pounds.

   _____

▶ **Rewrite the sentences. Add an adjective before each underlined noun. Use an adjective that answers the question in parentheses ( ).**

5. The <u>apple</u> fell from the tree. (What color?)

   _____

6. There were <u>apples</u> on the tree. (How many?)

   _____

7. Fatima ate the <u>apple</u>. (What size?)

   _____

8. I cut the <u>apple</u> into slices. (What shape?)

   _____

School–Home Connection

Ask your child to make a list of things in your home. Help him or her think of an adjective to describe each noun. The adjectives should tell what kind or how many.

Practice Book
© Harcourt • Grade 3

Name _____

▶ **Read the Spelling Words. Write each word in the group where it belongs.**

Words with *er*

1. _____
2. _____
3. _____
4. _____
5. _____

Words with *ir*

6. _____
7. _____
8. _____

Words with *ur*

9. _____
10. _____
11. _____

Words with *or*

12. _____
13. _____

Words with *ear*

14. _____
15. _____

Spelling Words

1. word
2. girl
3. burn
4. work
5. hurt
6. verse
7. purse
8. clerk
9. earth
10. perfect
11. first
12. pearl
13. answer
14. person
15. thirsty

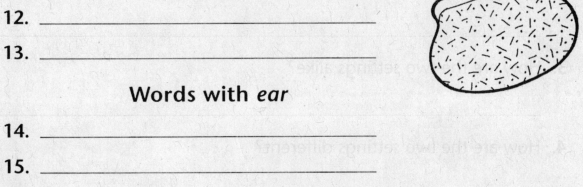

School–Home Connection

Read labels on food containers or clothing with your child. Find words with the *r*- Controlled vowels (*er, ir, ur, or, ear*) and write them down. Discuss the spelling of these words.

141

Practice Book
© Harcourt • Grade 3

▶ **Read the two story beginnings. Then write the answers to the questions.**

Story Beginning 1

    Lin stood in the kitchen waiting for her older brother, Aki. She turned on the light so she could see in the dark green kitchen. Then she opened the cabinet by the sink. Everything they needed was there. She pulled out yellow sponges, a bottle of liquid soap, washcloths, and a bottle of window cleaner. Aki came down the kitchen stairs with two buckets. Now, they were ready for a car wash.

Story Beginning 2

    Angela watered the flowers on the kitchen table. Her sister, Georgette, put the clean dishes away. After Georgette was done, it was time for their checkers game. Every day after they cleaned up the kitchen, they played checkers on the kitchen table. Angela thought that the bright yellow kitchen kept her focused and alert.

1. How are the two main characters alike?

_____

_____

2. How are the two families different?

_____

3. How are the two settings alike?

_____

4. How are the two settings different?

_____

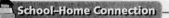

School–Home Connection

Help the student compare and contrast two things that are in the room. Ask how these things are alike. How are they different?

142

Name _____

▶ **In each sentence below, you will find a word with the /ûr/ sound. Circle that word and underline the letters that stand for the /ûr/ sound.**

1. My baby cousin just got his first tooth.

2. The car swerved to miss the hole in the road.

3. Each person who came received a free book.

4. Sasha plays third base on our softball team.

5. Li's new shirt is black and red.

6. Ms. Sanchez gave the class a stern look.

7. I was careful not to burn myself on the hot stove.

8. That baseball card is worth much more than

   I paid for it.

9. A strange car turned into the driveway.

10. The panting dog was very thirsty.

School–Home Connection

Have the student pronounce all the words with the underlined letter combinations *er*, *ir*, and *ur*. Then help him or her make up a story using those words.

143

▶ **Part A. Complete each sentence with one of the Vocabulary Words in the box.**

scolding	console	drowsy
glancing	heroic	burden

1. Two heavy piles of clothes are a _____ to carry.

2. A sleepy child looks _____.

3. A person with courage can be _____.

4. One reason for hugging people is to _____ them when they are feeling bad.

5. When someone looks quickly around a room, he or she is _____.

6. If I talk sternly to a child, I am probably _____ him or her.

▶ **Part B. Write an answer to each question.**

7. Why would you be **glancing** around in a restaurant?

_____

8. Why might you feel **drowsy**?

_____

School-Home Connection

Ask the student to talk about when a lifeguard might be *heroic*. Ask him or her to describe the heroic action.

▶ As you read "Two Bear Cubs," fill in the graphic organizer with details about how Older Brother and Younger Brother are alike and different. Then answer the questions.

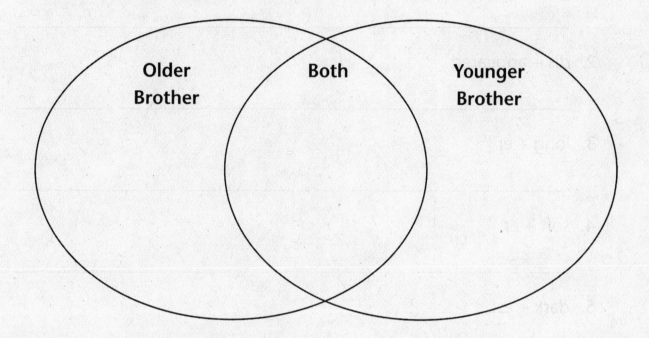

Older Brother   Both   Younger Brother

1. How is Older Brother different from Younger Brother?

   _____

   _____

2. How are Younger Brother and Older Brother alike?

   _____

   _____

▶ On a separate sheet of paper, summarize the selection. Use the graphic organizer to help you.

▶ **Form a word from each root word and each prefix or suffix. Then write a sentence for each word that you made.**

1. dis + agree

_____

2. dis + appeared

_____

3. long + er

_____

4. soft + er

_____

5. dark + est

_____

6. strong + est

_____

7. quick + ly

_____

Practice Book
© Harcourt • Grade 3

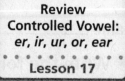

Name _____

▶ **Read each question. Circle the words in each question that have the letter combinations _er_, _ir_, _ur_, _ear_, and _or_. Then circle the word that answers that question.**

1. Which animal has fur and searches for nuts?

   a spider   an alligator   a squirrel

2. Who works to help people feel healthy?

   an actor   a nurse   a tailor

3. What is less than thirty-two?

   thirty-five   thirty-one   thirty-eight

4. Which animal might live beneath a fern and crawl through the dirt?

   a blackbird   an earthworm   a tiger

5. Which word names a person who sails on the sea?

   learner   tractor   sailor

6. Which could help you survive a cold night outside in early January?

   doing a crossword puzzle   burning wood   watching birds

School–Home Connection
Have the student tell you how he or she knew which were the correct answers.

147

Practice Book
© Harcourt • Grade 3

► **Write the form of each adjective that compares two things. Then write the form that compares three or more things.**

1. playful _____

2. funny _____

3. afraid _____

4. important _____

5. high _____

6. exciting _____

► **Rewrite each sentence correctly.**

7. The raccoon was small than the fox.

_____

8. Today's sunset was lovely than yesterday's sunset.

_____

9. That cliff was the most steep one I have ever climbed.

_____

10. The river was more deeper than the stream.

_____

School–Home Connection

With your child, take turns writing sentences that compare things in your home. (Examples: *This plant is taller than that one. That is the biggest bowl in the house.*)

Practice Book
· © Harcourt • Grade 3

Name _____

▶ Write the Spelling Words on cards. Lay them down and read them.

1. Circle the root word in each Spelling Word.
2. If the Spelling Word has a root word that ends with a consonant, write it in the correct part of the chart.
3. If the Spelling Word has a root word that ends with a vowel, write it in the other part of the chart.

Spelling Words

1. nicer
2. finest
3. useful
4. bigger
5. really
6. nicest
7. faster
8. lonely
9. quickly
10. careful
11. smaller
12. playful
13. biggest
14. slowly
15. thankful

Root Words That End with a Consonant	Root Words That End with a Vowel
1. _____	10. _____
2. _____	11. _____
3. _____	12. _____
4. _____	13. _____
5. _____	14. _____
6. _____	15. _____
7. _____	
8. _____	
9. _____	

School–Home Connection

Have your child retell a familiar short story as you write it down. Then have him or her circle all of the words that have the suffixes -er, -est, -ly, and -ful.

149

Practice Book
© Harcourt • Grade 3

Name _____

▶ **Read the story. Circle the letter of the best answer to each question. Underline the clues in the story that helped you answer the first question.**

Allie's Wheels

"I can't get this go-cart to work," Allie cried. She put down the wheel she had been trying to fit on the cart. "I'm tired of trying!"

Her mother picked up the wheel. "It will be fine. You just have to keep at it."

"But it's ugly," Allie said. "And I can't fix it!" She ran out of the garage and into her bedroom.

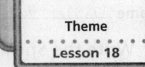

That night, Allie could not sleep. She thought about her go-cart. Slowly, she began to think of ways to make it better. She figured out how to attach the wheels so they would not fall off. She decided to paint the go-cart so it would not look so plain. In the morning, she hurried to the garage. Before her mother was up, Allie was hard at work. When her mother came into the garage, she was surprised. "Wow, Allie, your go-cart looks amazing!" she exclaimed.

"And look," Allie said, driving it out of the garage. "I've got wheels!"

---

1. What is the theme of this story?

   A It is easy to make a go-cart.

   B Even if something is hard to do, keep trying and you may do it.

   C Stop trying if something is difficult to do.

   D Having wheels is amazing.

2. What is a clue that helped tell what the theme is?

   A Allie could not sleep.

   B Her mother picked up the wheel.

   C Allie could not fix the go-cart.

   D Allie was hard at work.

150

▶ **Read the story. Circle the words with the suffixes
-er and *-est*. On the lines below, list those words
and write their root words beside them.**

Twila and Carlos walked along the beach. "Hey!" shouted Twila. "Look at
this rock. It is the shiniest rock I have ever seen!"

Carlos held out his hand. "This rock is shinier," he said. "It is also bigger."

Twila frowned. "My rock is nicer than yours," she said. "It is pointier, too."

"I do not like pointy rocks," said Carlos. "I like round rocks. Mine is
rounder than yours."

"Well," said Twila. "I do not like round rocks. I like red rocks. Mine is
redder than yours."

"Mine is the reddest!" shouted Carlos.

"Children," called their mother. "Why are you both shouting? You are
being the noisiest, silliest children I have ever seen."

1. _____

2. _____

3. _____

4. _____

5. _____

6. _____

7. _____

8. _____

9. _____

10. _____

School–Home Connection

Have the student make a list of five *-er* words
and five *-est* words.

151

Name _____

▶ **Use the Vocabulary Words from the box
below to complete the sentences.**

glorious	memory	crept
ruined	streak	yanked

1. If you are looking at something _____,

   then it must be very beautiful.

2. He _____ the rope,

   and pulled the basket out of the water.

3. The cat _____ slowly across

   the grass as it watched the bird.

4. Our rocket ship was _____

   when it landed on its side.

5. The plane left a lovely white _____

   when it flew over the mountain peak.

6. My favorite _____ is of my kitten

   playing with yarn.

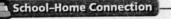
School–Home Connection
Help the student write a sentence of his or her
own with one of the Vocabulary Words.

152

Practice Book
© Harcourt • Grade 3

Name _____

▶ As you read "Me and Uncle Romie," fill in the graphic organizer to understand the story structure and theme. Use the page numbers to find what goes in each box.

Section 1 pages 90, 91

Characters	Setting
James, Uncle Romie, Aunt Nanette	

Section 2 pages 90, 98 Plot

Problem

Section 3 pages 91, 93, 94, 98, 99, 101, 103, 104, 105, 106

Events

Section 4 pages 100, 103

Solution

Theme

Practice Book
© Harcourt • Grade 3

▶ These directions tell how to make a paper airplane. Add a time-order word from the box to each step. Write the word on the line.

second   first   next   third   finally

How to Make a Paper Airplane

1. _____, take a piece of paper.

2. _____, fold down one end of the paper to meet the middle. Do the same with the other end. You will have a sharp point at one end of the paper.

3. _____, fold down the remaining sides of the paper. You will have an even sharper point at the same end.

4. _____, fold the edges back over so that the slanted edges are together.

5. _____, you are ready to fly your plane. Turn it over, place your fingers on the bottom edge, and let it glide through the air.

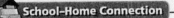
Practice Book
© Harcourt • Grade 3

Name _____

▶ **Read the story. Find the words with incorrect suffixes. Cross out those words. Then choose the correctly spelled words from the Word Box below, and write them above the words you crossed out.**

carefully	sternly	loudly	happiest	worriedly
playful	respectful	joyfully	higher	beautiful

It was a beautier day. The Outdoor Club members hiked up the mountain. Viya was the happier of all. She was going to hike highest than she had ever hiked before. She hiked carefulest, though. She did not want to fall.

Suddenly, Sven gave a shout. "I see a bear," he cried worriedful.

"Everyone start singing loudful," said Ms. Packer. "That will scare the bear away."

"Look," called Viya joyfulest. "The bear has two cubs. Oh, they are so playly!"

"They are still bears," said Ms. Packer sternest. "They are wild animals and we need to be respectest of them."

Then Ms. Packer led the Outdoor Club members back to camp.

School–Home Connection

Have the student add two sentences to the story. Each sentence should contain at least one word with the suffix -er, -est, -ly, or -ful.

155

Practice Book
© Harcourt • Grade 3

▶ **Use the articles *a*, *an*, and *the* to write two singular forms of each plural noun.**

Examples: birds: a bird, the bird

icy roads: an icy road, the icy road

1. skyscrapers _____

2. elevators _____

3. rooftops _____

4. noisy trains _____

5. escalators _____

6. shops _____

7. airports _____

8. excited boys _____

9. red cars _____

▶ **Write a sentence for each article. Circle the article, and underline the noun that it introduces.**

10. a   _____

11. an   _____

12. the   _____

Practice Book
© Harcourt • Grade 3

Name _____

▶ **Sort and write the Spelling Words with the prefixes *un-* *re-* and *dis-*.**

Words with Prefix *un-*

1. _____
2. _____
3. _____
4. _____
5. _____

Words with Prefix *re-*

6. _____
7. _____
8. _____
9. _____
10. _____
11. _____
12. _____

Words with Prefix *dis-*

13. _____
14. _____
15. _____

Spelling Words

1. undo
2. redo
3. dislike
4. react
5. refill
6. uneasy
7. reread
8. unlike
9. remove
10. dishonest
11. unhappy
12. rebuild
13. displease
14. uncover
15. rewrite

School–Home Connection

With your child write as many words with the prefixes *un, re,* and *dis* as you can. Use a dictionary to check your spelling.

157

▶ **Read the story. Then circle the letter of the best answer to each question.**

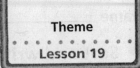

Nara the cat loved to daydream. She dreamed of living in a palace. She dreamed of wonderful meals and a servant to brush her fur. When her owner came near her, she hissed at him. She did not want to play. She just wanted to daydream.

The boy grew up and moved away, so Nara went to a new home. Nobody ever talked to her there. Nobody came to play with her, either. She had time to daydream, but she was not happy. She missed her old home. "I wish I had paid more attention to my owner," she thought. "We could have had fun. Now I am alone. My dreams were only dreams. Oh, why was I so foolish?"

1. What did Nara do instead of playing?

   A She ate and ate.

   B She ran away.

   C She slept in the sunshine.

   D She dreamed of a different place.

2. How did Nara feel about her new home?

   A She was scared and nervous.

   B She was unhappy.

   C She was happy and content.

   D She was cold and tired.

3. What is the theme of the story?

   A Try to enjoy the life you have.

   B Daydreams are better than real life.

   C Always try to live in a palace.

   D Cats have unusual habits.

School–Home Connection

Talk about a story you have read with the student. What message did the author try to teach in the story?

158

Name _____

▶ Find the *un-* words in the Word Search. Look up,
down, and across. Circle the words you find.

u	j	u	n	c	o	v	e	r	l	i	a
n	u	s	u	n	p	l	a	n	n	e	d
s	a	t	r	c	l	a	i	e	o	n	m
u	n	c	o	o	k	e	d	w	u	a	n
r	u	p	v	w	r	q	e	z	n	h	u
e	n	u	n	c	r	o	s	s	h	n	n
s	d	l	t	o	h	r	u	n	a	r	r
f	o	m	b	r	t	f	n	l	p	i	e
l	i	h	a	i	g	p	w	a	p	o	a
e	u	n	r	o	l	l	i	n	y	e	d
u	n	l	o	c	k	t	s	o	r	b	f
x	t	o	k	d	y	v	e	u	k	m	s
e	y	b	v	i	u	n	e	a	t	e	n
u	n	a	b	l	e	u	n	c	a	p	j
u	n	c	o	m	m	o	n	x	c	w	a

🚌 **School–Home Connection**

With the student, think of things a person
might do around their home that are spelled
with the prefix *un-*. Write them in a list.

159

Practice Book
© Harcourt • Grade 3

▶ **Write the Vocabulary Word from the box that best fits with the other words in each group.**

swift	vain	overheard
suggested	enormous	exclaimed

1. shouted

   loud

   _____

2. listened

   secret

   _____

3. stuck-up

   proud

   _____

4. huge

   large

   _____

5. fast

   run

   _____

6. asked

   offered

   _____

▶ **Complete each sentence.**

7. **Vain** people look in the mirror because _____

_____

8. **Swift** runners would win races because _____

_____

9. An **enormous** sandwich would be hard to eat because _____

_____

10. If you **overheard** a secret, you should _____

_____

School–Home Connection

With the student, name an animal that is enormous. Then name an animal that is swift.

Name _____

▶ Fill in the chart with information from the story. Since there are many characters, list only the five main characters. At the bottom of the page, write a summary of the theme.

Section 1

Characters	Setting

Plot

Section 2

Problem

Section 3

Important Events

Section 4

Solution

Theme

▶ Use the information from the chart above to write a summary of the story on a separate sheet of paper.

Practice Book
© Harcourt • Grade 3

▶ **The directions below are out of order. Rewrite them on the lines that follow. Use the time-order words to figure out the correct order.**

How to Teach a Dog to "Sit"

Third, gently press down on your dog's bottom until the dog sits.

Second, say "Sit" in a firm voice.

Then repeat the lesson until your dog sits on its own.

First, be sure your dog is standing up and facing you.

Next, say "Good dog!" and give the dog a nice treat.

Finally, remember to always take very good care of your dog.

_____

_____

_____

_____

_____

_____

_____

_____

_____

_____

School-Home Connection

Have the student write directions for
something that he or she does every day.

162

Practice Book
© Harcourt • Grade 3

Name _____

▶ **Part A**

Make spelling words by joining *re-*, *un-*, or *dis-*
with one of the base words. Write the spelling
words on the lines.

re-	honest
	easy
un-	write
	act
dis-	please
	happy

1. _____   4. _____

2. _____   5. _____

3. _____   6. _____

▶ **Part B**

Write sentences, using the spelling words you used in Part A. Use at
least two spelling words in each sentence.

7. _____

_____

8. _____

_____

9. _____

_____

School–Home Connection

With the student, think of other words with
the prefixes *re-*, *un-*, and *dis-*. Write the words
in a list.

163

Practice Book
© Harcourt • Grade 3

▶ **Rewrite each sentence. Use the correct form of the verb in parentheses ( ).**

1. An egg (hatch/hatches) in the nest.

   _____

2. The ducklings (follow/follows) their mother.

   _____

3. The farmer (hurry/hurries) home.

   _____

4. Mice (scurry/scurries) around the barn.

   _____

5. We (milk/milks) the cows every morning.

   _____

6. She (drive/drives) the big tractor.

   _____

7. Jessica (help/helps) my brother dry dishes.

   _____

8. They (clean/cleans) the kitchen.

   _____

School–Home Connection

Work with your child to write four sentences, using action verbs in the present tense. Ask him or her to underline each verb and write S (singular) or P (plural) above each subject.

Name _____

▶ **Read the words in the Word Box. Write each word in the correct column. Then answer the questions.**

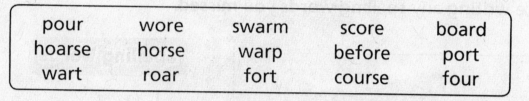

pour	wore	swarm	score	board
hoarse	horse	warp	before	port
wart	roar	fort	course	four

r-controlled vowel pattern:				
or	*ore*	*our*	*ar*	*oar*

1. How are the words *pour* and *hour* alike and different?

_____

_____

2. What other words use *ore* to make the /ôr/ sound?

_____

_____

3. What is one more word with *ar* that stands for /ôr/? What is one

   word with *ar* that does not stand for /ôr/?

_____

School–Home Connection

Ask the student to think of one more word for
each column of the chart.

Practice Book
© Harcourt • Grade 2

Name _____

▶ Fold the paper along the dotted line. As each
spelling word is read aloud, write it in the blank.
Then unfold your paper and check your work.
Practice writing any spelling words you missed.

1. _____

2. _____

3. _____

4. _____

5. _____

6. _____

7. _____

8. _____

9. _____

10. _____

11. _____

12. _____

13. _____

14. _____

15. _____

Spelling Words

1. form
2. wore
3. fourth
4. soar
5. warn
6. perfect
7. girl
8. burn
9. work
10. earth
11. bigger
12. finest
13. lonely
14. refill
15. dishonest

Name _____

Review
r-Controlled Vowel:
/ûr/er, ir, ur,
ir, or, ear
Lesson 20

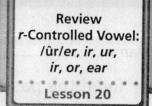

▶ **Circle the word in each clue that has the /ûr/ sound. Then write the circled words in the crossword puzzle.**

Across

1. I like the purple pants.

4. Help me search for my dog.

6. Make a left turn.

7. Have you memorized all the spelling words?

Down

1. That is a pretty pearl necklace.

2. We will learn about vowels today.

3. I want to buy new shirts.

5. Chopping wood is hard work.

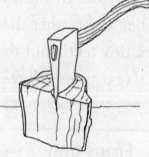

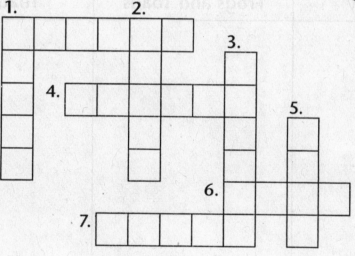

Practice Book
© Harcourt • Grade 3

Name _____

▶ **Read the passage. Then compare and contrast frogs and toads by completing the chart.**

Frogs and Toads

Although frogs and toads are similar, they are also quite different. Frogs and toads are both amphibians. They live both in water and on land, hatching from eggs as tadpoles. Both creatures can make sounds by passing air through their throats. Both also have special glands on their skin that make their bodies taste bad to predators.

Frogs, however, have moist, smooth skin, while toads have drier, bumpy skin. In addition, frogs have longer back legs and can jump higher and farther than toads can jump. But toads can walk. Frogs also have tiny teeth, but toads have no teeth at all.

Next time you see a frog, stop and look. It could be a toad!

Frogs only	Frogs and Toads	Toads only

School–Home Connection

Have the student name two of his or her favorite animals and write sentences comparing and contrasting them.

Practice Book
© Harcourt • Grade 3

▶ **Read this part of a student's rough draft. Then answer the questions that follow.**

(1) There was an art show at the library yesterday. (2) Children displayed their art. (3) I showed two paintings. (4) They were the largest ones in the room. (5) There were also _____ photographs and a black sculpture. (6) The sculpture was interesting than the photographs.

1. Which sentence uses the correct form of an adjective that compares?
   A Sentence 3
   B Sentence 4
   C Sentence 5
   D Sentence 6

2. Which adjective needs the word *more* before it?
   A two (Sentence 3)
   B largest (Sentence 4)
   C black (Sentence 5)
   D interesting (Sentence 6)

3. Which adjective could be written before *Children* in Sentence 2?
   A Many
   B One
   C Hundred
   D Each

4. Which adjective that tells *what kind* could fill in the blank in Sentence 5?
   A biggest
   B tiniest
   C small
   D some

5. Which sentence has an adjective that tells *what color*?
   A Sentence 1
   B Sentence 3
   C Sentence 4
   D Sentence 5

6. Which of these sentences does NOT have an adjective?
   A Sentence 2
   B Sentence 3
   C Sentence 4
   D Sentence 5

Name _____

▶ **Circle the word in each row that is spelled incorrectly. Then write the correct word on the line.**

1. lovely   loveler   loveliest   _____

2. fast   faster   fastiest   _____

3. nicer   niciest   nicely   _____

4. biggier   biggest   big   _____

5. clumsy   clumsest   clumsier   _____

6. hardder   hardly   hardest   _____

7. quietly   quietier   quietest   _____

8. softtest   softly   softer   _____

9. sillyer   silliest   silly   _____

10. gentle   gentler   gentliest   _____

School–Home Connection

Have the student think of a synonym for *lovely* that has the suffix *-ful*. Then help him or her think of synonyms for *happy* that have the suffixes *-ly* and *-ful*.

170

Name _____

▶ **Underline the prefix or suffix in each word.**
Then write the meaning of the word.

Word   **Definition**

1. repay   _____

2. joyful   _____

3. unwrap   _____

4. colder   _____

5. disrespect _____

6. funniest   _____

7. unable   _____

8. eventful   _____

9. cleverly   _____

10. happiest _____

School–Home Connection

With the student, think of other prefixes or
suffixes you could add to each root word in
the first column.

171

Practice Book
© Harcourt • Grade 3

Name

▶ Use the clues to unscramble the letters. Then
write the Vocabulary Word and definition.

| versions | rehearse | mandatory |
| criticize | immerse | dialogue |

1. Soccer practice is ytdnamaro if you want to play in the game.

_____

2. When you rrheeesa for the play, make sure you say your lines clearly.

_____

3. Many painters sketch out different nsovreis before they begin painting.

_____

4. When teachers zicitrcei your work, they give you suggestions to

improve it.

_____

5. The best way to learn about something is to emmeisr yourself in it.

_____

6. The eulaodig in a book can tell you a lot about a character's traits.

_____

School–Home Connection
Have the student make up other sentences
using the Vocabulary Words.

172

Practice Book
© Harcourt • Grade 3

▶ **Circle the word that matches the definition.
Then underline the other words that are real words.**

1. to take off the cover

    discover   uncover   recover

2. to play again

    replay   unplay   display

3. to visit again

    disvisit   unvisit   revisit

4. to not like something

    unlike   dislike   relike

5. to type again

    retype   distype   untype

6. not popular

    repopular   dispopular   unpopular

7. to not obey

    disobey   reobey   unobey

173

▶ Read this part of a student's rough draft.
Then answer the questions that follow.

> (1) Luke interviews his mother for a newsletter at school. (2) He asks his mother questions and writes down a answers. (3) _____ questions are about his mother's job. (4) Luke's mother is a engineer. (5) She plans bridges, and people builds them. (6) Students enjoy the report that Luke writes.

1. In which sentence should the article be changed to *an*?
   A Sentence 1
   B Sentence 2
   C Sentence 4
   D Sentence 6

2. Which word could fill in the blank in Sentence 3?
   A A
   B An
   C The
   D Writes

3. Which sentence has a plural noun with an article that does NOT agree?
   A Sentence 1
   B Sentence 2
   C Sentence 4
   D Sentence 6

4. Which of these action verbs does NOT agree with its subject?
   A interviews (Sentence 1)
   B writes (Sentence 2)
   C plans (Sentence 5)
   D builds (Sentence 5)

5. Which sentence has only one action verb?
   A Sentence 1
   B Sentence 2
   C Sentence 5
   D Sentence 6

6. Which sentence has a plural subject and an action verb that agrees?
   A Sentence 1
   B Sentence 2
   C Sentence 4
   D Sentence 6

► **Read the story. Then answer the questions.**

Olivia wanted to be a singer more than anything in the world.

"Your voice is too scratchy and low," Carl said during choir practice. "It sounds like you ate a cactus!"

Olivia tried to ignore him. Her voice did not sound like the other singers' voices. Carl's voice was smooth and not too high or too low.

"I have new songs today," Miss Cuttle announced to the class. "Each person will get a song to sing that suits his or her voice."

Olivia was nervous. She wondered what song could suit her rough voice. Olivia anxiously walked up to Miss Cuttle. "I know I have problems with my voice," Olivia said quietly.

Miss Cuttle grinned. "I have a special song for you. Many famous jazz singers had voices just like yours. I think a jazz song will be perfect."

1. What is Olivia's voice like? _____

2. Why is Olivia nervous? _____

   _____

3. Why does Miss Cuttle choose a jazz song for Olivia? _____

   _____

   _____

4. What is one possible theme for the story? _____

   _____

   _____

School–Home Connection

Have the student explain which story clues he or she used to determine the story's theme.

175

Practice Book
© Harcourt • Grade 3

Name _____

▶ **Follow the directions to draw a picture in the space below.**

First, draw a square.

Second, draw a large circle inside the square.

Third, draw two triangles inside the circle.

Fourth, draw a star below the triangles.

Last, write the names of all the shapes you drew below the picture.

Shapes: _____

Practice Book
© Harcourt • Grade 3

Vowel Variants
/ōō/ oo, ew, ue,
ui; /ŏŏ/ oo

Lesson 21

Name _____

▶ **Read the Spelling Words. Then write each word in the group where it belongs.**

Words with /ōō/ as in *booth*

1. _____
2. _____
3. _____
4. _____
5. _____
6. _____
7. _____
8. _____
9. _____
10. _____

Words with /ŏŏ/ as in *cook*

11. _____
12. _____
13. _____
14. _____

▶ **Write the word that is left on the line.**

15. _____

Spelling Words

1. threw
2. cool
3. foot
4. cook
5. bruise
6. hook
7. tool
8. brook
9. booth
10. school
11. choose
12. balloon
13. cartoon
14. afternoon
15. understood

School–Home Connection

Talk about the different vowel sounds in *booth* and *cook*. Discuss with your child other words that share the same vowel sounds. Practice spelling aloud words with the ōō and ŏŏ sounds.

177

Practice Book
© Harcourt • Grade 3

Name _____

▶ **Read the passage and answer the questions.**

> Roald Amundsen (1872–1928) was a polar explorer from Norway. He is best known for leading the first successful expedition to the South Pole, which lasted from 1910 to 1912.
>
> Before leading his own expedititons, Amundsen was a member of the Belgian Antarctic Expedition (1897-1899). This journey taught Amundsen how to survive the harshness of Antarctica. He would later use this knowledge for his own expeditions.
>
> In 1910, Amundsen and his expedition set out for the South Pole. On his ship *Fram*, whose name means "forward," Amundsen and his crew first arrived at the edge of the Ross Ice Shelf. There he established a base camp, from which he led his crew across the Antarctic ice. Amundsen and his crew arrived at the South Pole on December 14, 1911. Then they faced the long, dangerous journey back. It took until March 1, 1912, to complete that trek and let the rest of the world hear the news of their accomplishment.

1. What happened before Amundsen led his own expeditions?

_____

2. When did Amundsen begin his journey to the South Pole?

_____

3. When did Amundsen and his crew arrive at the South Pole?

_____

4. What are some time-order words used in this passage?

_____

Practice Book
© Harcourt • Grade 3

▶ Circle the /o͞o/ word in each riddle. Then
unscramble the letters to make a /o͞o/ word
that solves the riddle. Write the answer word
on the line.

What Am I?

1. I am a place where you might see a kangaroo.

   ozo _____

2. You do this when you eat food.

   wche _____

3. I am a building with many classrooms.

   socohl _____

4. It's hard to eat noodles while using me.

   nospo _____

5. Someone did this to make a cartoon.

   rewd _____

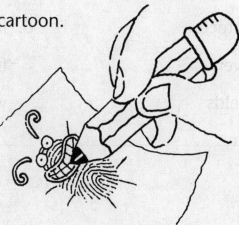

School–Home Connection

Work with the student to create another /o͞o/
riddle with *moon*, *flew*, or *new*.

179

Practice Book
© Harcourt • Grade 3

▶ **Pick a word from the Word Box that best fits with each group of words. Write the word on the line.**

permanently	drifts	dim
scarce	shelters	absence

1. weak

   faint

   not bright

   _____

2. few

   rare

   hard to find

   _____

3. protects

   covers

   shields

   _____

4. gone

   missing

   away

   _____

5. carried along by water

   floats

   to move slowly

   _____

6. lasting

   forever

   without change

   _____

School–Home Connection

Have the student use his or her hands to act out the word **drifts**. Then ask the student to do something to show the **absence** of light in a room.

Practice Book
© Harcourt • Grade 3

Name _____

▶ As you read "Antarctic Ice," fill in the graphic
organizer with events in time order. Then answer
the questions below the graphic organizer.

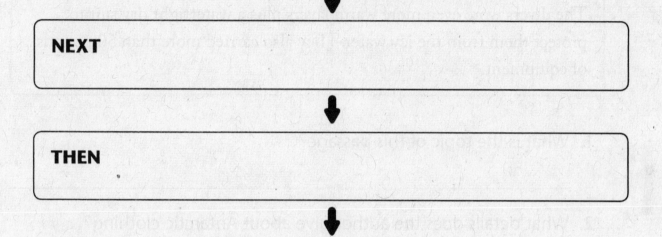

FIRST Antarctic sea animals are waiting for summer to
arrive.

⬇

NEXT

⬇

THEN

⬇

LAST

1. What is happening at the beginning of "Antarctic Ice"?

   _____

   _____

2. What happens to the days soon after the sun returns?

   _____

   _____

▶ On a separate sheet of paper, summarize the selection. Use the
graphic organizer to help you.

Practice Book
© Harcourt • Grade 3

▶ **Read the passage below from "Living at the Bottom of the World." Then answer each question.**

> Because the weather outside was cold and windy, I wore special clothing issued by the U.S. Antarctic Program—thermal underwear, socks, boots, a hat, a waterproof coat, and gloves. Anytime I was near the water, I wore a bright-orange float-coat that worked as a life preserver. The divers wore even more warm layers plus a watertight dry suit to protect them from the icy water. They also carried more than 50 pounds of equipment.

1. What is the topic of this passage?

   _____

2. What details does the author give about Antarctic clothing?

   _____

   _____

3. Why did the scientists and divers wear special clothing?

   _____

   _____

4. What kind of clothes did divers wear?

   _____

   _____

5. What do you think is the author's message?

   _____

School–Home Connection

Discuss with the student other information that might be added to this passage.

182

Practice Book
© Harcourt • Grade 3

▶ Unscramble each /o͞o/ or /o͝o/ mystery word.
Then use it to complete the sentence.

1. **leub**   Saul painted his toy boat bright _____.

2. **olop**   He sailed his boat in a small _____ of

water.

3. **sciure**   He said his boat was going on a _____.

4. **otto**   I heard his boat _____ and whistle.

5. **nwek**   Then it was quiet, and I _____

something had happened.

6. **okol**   "Let me take a _____," I said.

7. **ugle**   I fixed the broken boat with a little bit of

_____.

8. **godo**   In no time, Saul's boat was as _____

as ever.

9. **wleb**   The wind _____ the boat across the

water.

10. **fenatrono** It had been a nice, sunny _____.

School–Home Connection

Have the student choose two of the mystery
words and use them in oral sentences.

183

Practice Book
© Harcourt • Grade 3

▶ Circle the form of the verb *be* in each sentence.
Then write whether each links the subject to
words that tell *what* or *where*.

1. Some seals are white. _____

2. The penguin chick was fuzzy. _____

3. You were on the shore. _____

4. That shark is near a whale. _____

5. I am with my parents. _____

6. They are scientists. _____

▶ Rewrite each sentence, using a correct form of the verb *be*. Then
write *S* above each singular subject and *P* above each plural subject.

7. Those fish _____ small and silver.

_____

8. We _____ close to the beaver's dam.

_____

9. He _____ in a wooden boat.

_____

10. The river _____ full of life.

_____

School–Home Connection

Have your child write sentences about his
or her favorite season. Ask him or her to
use singular and plural subjects and to write
sentences that tell *what* and *where*.

Vowel Variants
/ô/ o, au, aw, a(l),
au(gh), ough

Lesson 22

Name _____

▶ Read the Spelling Words. Listen for the vowel sound in each word. Sort the words and write them where they belong.

Words Beginning with a Vowel Sound

1. _____
2. _____
3. _____
4. _____

Words with a Vowel Sound in the Middle

5. _____
6. _____
7. _____
8. _____
9. _____
10. _____
11. _____
12. _____
13. _____
14. _____
15. _____

Spelling Words

1. ought
2. soft
3. yawn
4. walk
5. long
6. also
7. thaw
8. lost
9. cause
10. taught
11. pause
12. straw
13. false
14. author
15. almost

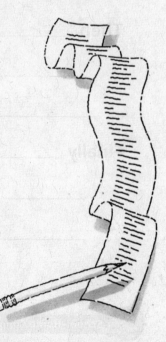

School–Home Connection

With your child, make a list of words that have the same vowel sound you hear in the word *ball*. Discuss the spelling of each word.

185

▶ **Read the article. Then write the main events in order.**

Fishing With Feet

One kind of bat eats fish. The way the bat catches its dinner is amazing. First, it flies very low over the water. Next, it dangles its hind legs in the water. The legs look like a tasty treat to the fish, so the fish comes closer. Then, the bat snags a small fish with its sharp toenails. The fish may struggle, but the bat holds tight. Finally, the bat pulls the fish out of the water and eats it.

First _____

_____

_____

Next _____

_____

_____

Then _____

_____

_____

Finally _____

_____

_____

Practice Book
© Harcourt • Grade 3

Name _____

▶ In the chart below, write a word from the Word
Box in the correct column. Some words might
belong in more than one column. Use the words that do
not belong in any column to answer the questions below.

ought	soar	caught	pause
clown	bought	cause	strong
author	cool	boil	taught

Words with /ô/ as *au*	Words with /ô/ as *ou*	Words with *gh*

1. How would a glass of lemonade feel on a hot summer day?

   _____

2. If you could lift a heavy load of books, what would you be?

   _____

3. What happens to water when it heats until bubbles appear?

   _____

4. What kind of person is very funny and usually wears a big red nose?

   _____

5. What does a bird do when it flies high into the air? _____

School–Home Connection

With the student, think of other words that
have /ô/ as *au*. Have him or her write the words
in sentences.

187

▶ **Write the Vocabulary Word from the box that goes with each explanation.**

effort	swoops	detail
fluttering	nocturnal	dozes

1. _____ Active at night

2. _____ An important point

3. _____ Flies quickly downward

4. _____ Trying hard

5. _____ Moving wings quickly

6. _____ Sleeps lightly

▶ **Answer the questions in complete sentences.**

7. If a bird **swoops**, does it move quickly or slowly?

_____

8. If you notice a **detail** in a painting, are you looking at only a part of it?

_____

9. If someone makes an **effort**, is he or she trying hard or not trying?

_____

10. When is a **nocturnal** animal likely to be active?

_____

11. Is it hard or easy to wake up someone who **dozes**?

_____

12. If a bird is **fluttering**, how are its wings moving?

_____

School–Home Connection

With the student, look outside for **nocturnal** animals and insects that might be **fluttering** around an outside light at night.

188

Name _____

▶ As you read "Bat Loves the Night," fill in the graphic organizer with the sequence of events in the narrative.

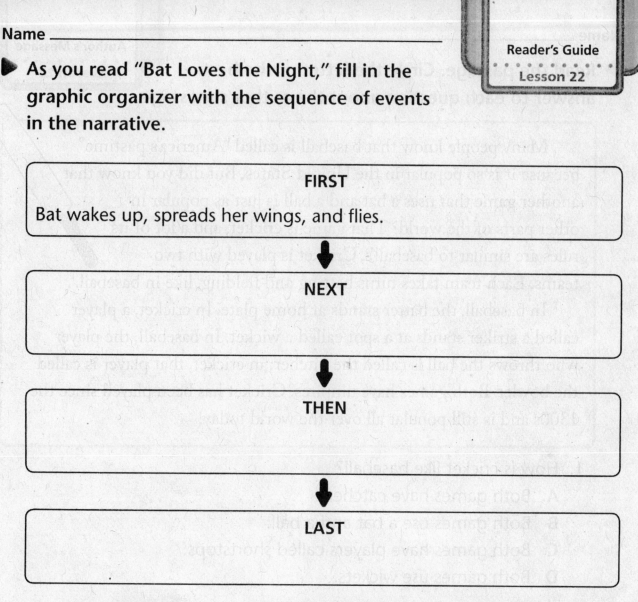

FIRST

Bat wakes up, spreads her wings, and flies.

⬇

NEXT

⬇

THEN

⬇

LAST

1. What happens to the moth after Bat bites it for the first time?

_____

2. What is the last thing Bat does in the narrative?

_____

▶ On a separate sheet of paper, summarize the selection. Use the graphic organizer to help you.

189

▶ **Read the passage. Circle the letter of the best answer to each question about the author's message.**

Many people know that baseball is called "America's pastime" because it is so popular in the United States. But did you know that another game that uses a bat and a ball is just as popular in other parts of the world? That game is cricket, and a lot of its rules are similar to baseball's. Cricket is played with two teams. Each team takes turns batting and fielding, like in baseball.

In baseball, the batter stands at home plate. In cricket, a player called a striker stands at a spot called a wicket. In baseball, the player who throws the ball is called the pitcher; in cricket, that player is called the bowler. Both games have umpires. Cricket has been played since the 1300s and is still popular all over the world today!

1. How is cricket like baseball?
   A Both games have catchers.
   B Both games use a bat and a ball.
   C Both games have players called shortstops.
   D Both games use wickets.

2. Which sentence is true?
   A Both cricket and baseball have pitchers.
   B Cricket uses umpires, but baseball does not.
   C Cricket is played with four teams; baseball is played with two.
   D Cricket has been played since the 1300's, but baseball was invented in the 1800s.

3. What was the author's message in this passage?
   A Cricket is popular in the United States.
   B Baseball players should play cricket instead.
   C Playing cricket or baseball is a good way to get in shape.
   D Cricket and baseball are alike and different in many ways.

School–Home Connection

Ask the student to point out some of the sentences that helped show the author's message in this selection.

190

Name _____

▶ **Write the words from the word box in the correct column. Then, find the /ô/ words in the word search below.**

bought	caught	taught
fought	ought	author
	thought	pause

/ô/ as *au(gh)*	/ô/ as *ough*
_____	_____
_____	_____
_____	_____
_____	_____

WORD SEARCH

B	F	T	A	U	G	H	T	X	A
D	P	A	U	S	E	I	H	U	A
F	Q	I	T	R	C	J	O	V	R
O	U	G	H	T	A	T	U	C	I
U	R	H	O	C	A	U	G	H	T
G	S	K	R	Z	W	E	H	U	N
H	M	B	O	U	G	H	T	A	W
T	G	E	O	H	K	N	A	L	T

191

Name _____

▶ **Rewrite the sentences. Add a helping verb to each one.**

1. I never studied mammals.

_____

2. We learn about bats.

_____

3. We go to the library.

_____

4. Butterflies see red, yellow, and green.

_____

5. A butterfly landed on that leaf.

_____

6. That butterfly laid 400 eggs.

_____

7. Butterflies fly only when they are warm.

_____

8. The librarian found a great book about butterflies.

_____

192

Name _____

▶ **Read the Spelling Words. Sort the words and write them where they belong.**

Words with *pre-*

1. _____
2. _____
3. _____
4. _____
5. _____

Words with *mis-*

6. _____
7. _____
8. _____
9. _____
10. _____
11. _____

Words with *in-*

12. _____
13. _____
14. _____
15. _____

Spelling Words

1. input
2. preset
3. misuse
4. inside
5. preview
6. incorrect
7. pretest
8. mislead
9. preheat
10. indoors
11. misplace
12. preschool
13. misread
14. mismatch
15. misspell

School–Home Connection

With your child, make a list of five words with the prefixes *pre-, mis-,* and *in-.* Then have your child circle the prefix in each word. Challenge him or her to use each word in a sentence.

193

Practice Book
© Harcourt • Grade 3

▶ **Read the passage. Look for cause and effect relationships as you read. Then answer the questions.**

Using Good Sense

Bats are amazing creatures. Not only are they the only flying mammals, but they also have great senses. Bats have strong senses of smell, hearing, and eyesight. Because of these great senses, bats are able to be active at night.

Bats use their hearing, vision, and sense of smell to find food in the dark. In fact, they can see better in the dark than in the daylight. Their strong sense of smell lets bats find ripe fruit. They use their sharp hearing to find other food sources, too, such as insects and fish.

Bats also use these strong senses to find other bats. They use their sense of smell to recognize their roost mates. Their great hearing helps them find their young.

1. What causes bats to be able to be active at night?

   _____

2. What is an effect of a bat's strong sense of hearing?

   _____

3. What causes bats to be able to find other bats?

   _____

4. What is an effect of a bat's strong sense of smell?

   _____

School–Home Connection

Read and discuss the passage with the student. Have him or her explain the cause and effect relationships in the text using words such as *so* and *because*.

194

Practice Book
© Harcourt • Grade 3

▶ Look at the words in the squares. Shade the
squares that have words with the prefix *pre-*,
mis-, or *in-* in front of a root word. Circle the
prefix in each word.

preheat	pretzel	misuse	preview
injure	mister	pretest	indoors
predator	misspell	miserable	insect
input	preschool	mislead	ink
missing	president	incorrect	mission

School-Home Connection

Have the student read the spelling words on
the page aloud. Then ask him or her to share
the meanings of the words with the prefix *pre-*.

Practice Book
© Harcourt • Grade 3

| fondness | decent | inherit |
| ridiculous | emotion | disgraceful |

▶ **Part A. Write the Vocabulary Word that matches each idea.**

1. _____ something silly or strange

2. _____ honest and good

3. _____ to receive something from someone else

4. _____ a liking or affection

5. _____ shameful or unacceptable

6. _____ a feeling such as happiness or anger

▶ **Part B. Answer each question about the Vocabulary Words.**

7. If someone's actions are **disgraceful**, should that person be

   embarrassed by or proud of that behavior?

   _____

8. Would a **decent** person be trustworthy or untrustworthy?

   _____

9. Would something **ridiculous** make you laugh or cry?

   _____

10. What kind of **emotion** would make you smile?

    _____

11. Would a mouse have a **fondness** for snakes or cheese?

    _____

12. If you **inherit** something, is it a gift or do you buy it?

    _____

School-Home Connection

Ask the student to give examples of things that
are ridiculous. Then ask him or her to name
several emotions and to tell which things cause
those feelings.

Practice Book
© Harcourt • Grade 3

Name _____

▶ As you read "Chestnut Cove," fill in the graphic organizer. Sometimes there may be more than one cause or effect for a single action. You may also find more than one cause and effect relationship in the story. Draw more boxes as you need them.

Section 1 page 233

Cause	→	Effect

| | | Effect |

Section 2 page 238

Cause	→	Effect

| | | Effect |

1. What was one cause you found in the story?

_____

_____

2. What effect or effects did this action have?

_____

_____

▶ On a separate sheet of paper, summarize the selection. Use the graphic organizer to help you.

Name _____

► **Choose the correct homophone to complete each sentence. Then write a sentence using the other homophone.**

1. blew / blue

   We painted my bedroom walls _____.

   _____

2. pear / pair

   I wore a new _____ of shoes to school today.

   _____

3. see / sea

   The sailor said there is nothing like being on the open _____.

   _____

4. nose / knows

   Do you think anyone _____ how to get there?

   _____

5. hair / hare

   She washes her _____ every night.

   _____

School-Home Connection

Have the student write homophones for *bee*, *won*, *knight*, *two*, and *their*.

Practice Book
© Harcourt • Grade 3

Name _____

► Read each of the words at the top of the
page. Then follow the directions below.

precook   mislead

invisible   preheat

mismatch   prepackage   misuse

1. Circle the word that means "to package before."

2. Draw a triangle around the word that means "not visible."

3. Underline the word that means "to cook before."

4. Draw a box around the word that means "to use badly."

5. Cross off the word the means "to lead wrongly."

6. Draw a star beside the word that means "to heat before."

7. Draw a zigzag line under the word that means "to match wrongly."

School–Home Connection

Have the student use the words *invisible*,
preheat, and *misdirect* in sentences. Then ask
him or her to tell you the meanings of each of
the prefixes.

199

Practice Book
© Harcourt • Grade 3

Name _____

▶ **Rewrite each sentence correctly, using the subject in parentheses ( ). Be sure that the verb in your sentence agrees with its new subject.**

Example: Glenda likes math. (My brothers)

My brothers like math.

1. I enter a writing contest. (George)

_____

2. The teachers judge the contest. (A teacher)

_____

3. One student wins the contest. (Two students)

_____

4. We like stories about animals. (You)

_____

5. She prefers true stories. (He)

_____

6. The princesses meet a prince. (The princess)

_____

7. We hurry home from school. (They)

_____

8. Our mother opens the front door. (We)

_____

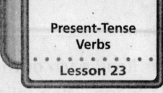
School–Home Connection

Write two sentences with present-tense verbs. Ask your child to rewrite the sentences, changing the subjects and making sure that the verbs agree with their new subjects.

200

Name _____

▶ **Read the Spelling Words. Sort the words and write them where they belong.**

Words Beginning with the /ə/ Sound

1. _upon_
2. _____
3. _____
4. _____
5. _____
6. _____
7. _____
8. _____
9. _____
10. _____
11. _____
12. _____

Spelling Words

1. upon
2. above
3. cover
4. apart
5. either
6. alike
7. awake
8. afraid
9. across
10. agree
11. ever
12. amount
13. ahead
14. alive
15. around

Words Ending with the /ər/ Sound

13. _cover_
14. _____
15. _____

School-Home Connection

Brainstorm with your child other words that have the schwa sound that you hear in *above* and *ever*. Discuss how to spell each word. Confirm each spelling in a dictionary.

201

▶ **Read the passage. Then answer the questions.**

> "Ha!" Keisha said. "I knew I could do it!" Keisha had just taught herself to ride her older brother, Ben's, bike. Ben had delivered papers for six months and made enough money to buy it. He told her not to ride the bike because she was too little and might break it. Since she was stubborn, Keisha secretly rode the bike when he was at oboe practice.
>
> One afternoon, Keisha left the bike on the driveway and went inside. Then she heard a loud crunch from outside. "Oh no!" she said. "The bike!" Sure enough, Mom had run over the bike with the car. Since the broken bike was Keisha's fault, she agreed to help Ben deliver newspapers on foot until he made enough money to buy a new bike.

1. What is the cause of Keisha secretly riding Ben's bike?

_____

2. What is the effect of Keisha leaving the bike on the driveway?

_____

3. What is the cause of Keisha helping Ben deliver newspapers?

_____

4. What is the effect of Ben delivering papers for six months?

_____

_____

School–Home Connection

Ask the student to identify the cause of Ben telling Keisha not to ride his bike.

Practice Book
© Harcourt • Grade 3

▶ **Read the incomplete sentences below. Underline the word that has the schwa sound and completes the sentence.**

1. If you do not understand the sentence, read _____. (ahead / slowly)

2. After the race, she needed to drink a lot of _____. (water / limeade)

3. The building in the _____ is the tallest. (background / center)

4. The school play was a huge _____.   (success / sellout)

5. A long time _____, my family lived in Italy. (back / ago)

6. My sister has special _____ because she is a runner.

   (outfits / sneakers)

7. They went _____ on vacation to the Grand Canyon. (away / quickly)

8. What was your _____ for being late? (excuse / reason)

9. She had to do her math homework _____ because she made too

   many mistakes. (twice / again)

10. Autumn is my favorite _____ because of the colorful leaves.

   (season / time)

School-Home Connection

Ask the student to identify the letters that
make the schwa sound in items #1 and #2.

203

Practice Book
© Harcourt • Grade 3

Name _____

▶ **Part A. Choose one Vocabulary Word from the box to complete each unfinished sentence below. Write the word on the line.**

| clutter | mentioned | remark |
| visible | beckoned | flustered |

Anna's mom entered her daughter's room. It was a mess! Anna's bed

was so covered with clothes, it was barely _____.

Anna's mom _____ that perhaps Anna should

clean her room if she wanted to play with her friends. Anna seemed

_____, but she did start putting things away. About an

hour later, Anna _____ to her mom to take a look. All

the _____ had been removed. Her mom was pleased

with the results. Anna was able to go out and play. As she ran out the

door, Anna heard her mom _____, "Good job!"

▶ **Part B. Write one or two sentences to answer each question.**

1. What might you show your friends if you *beckoned* for them to

   come see something?

   _____

   _____

2. How would you make sure you were *visible* if you were riding your

   bicycle at night?

   _____

   _____

School-Home Connection

Ask the student to think of three things that
would make them feel *flustered*.

204

Name _____

▶ As you read "Ramona Quimby, Age 8," think about events that cause other events to happen. Think about events that happen as a result of others. Write the causes and effects in the chart below.

Section 1 pages 262–263

Cause		Effect
Ramona is home sick from school.	➡	

Section 2 pages 264–267

Cause		Effect
	➡	

Section 3 pages 268–271

Cause		Effect
	➡	

1. How does Ramona choose to present her book report? _____

_____

2. What causes this to happen? _____

_____

▶ On a separate sheet of paper, summarize "Ramona Quimby, Age 8." Use the graphic organizer to help you.

205

▶ **Read the homophones in parentheses. Complete each sentence with the correct word.**

1. (hole, whole)   There is a big _____ in my old jeans.

   I can't believe I read the _____ thing!

2. (flew, flu)   A flock of birds just _____ by the window.

   Jisela missed school when she had the

   _____ .

3. (rains, reins)   When you go horseback riding,

   hold the _____ tightly.

   When it _____, the hiking trail gets muddy.

4. (meet, meat)   Beef and chicken are two types of _____ .

   I hope I get to _____ that movie star.

5. (There, Their)   _____ are colorful

   birds on the island.

   _____ beaks are red and yellow.

6. (write, right)   Caitlyn throws with her _____ hand.

   Beverly is going to _____ a poem for her

   mother.

School–Home Connection
Ask the student to come up with a homophone
and a sentence for the word *see.*

Name _____

▶ **Complete the riddles by filling in each blank with a word from the box. Then write the word on the second line, dividing it into syllables. Underline the syllable or syllables that make the schwa sound.**

sofa	mirror	imitate
cucumber	pizza	reporter

1. A green vegetable with seeds is a _____.

   _____

2. When you copy what someone says or does, you

   _____ that person.

   _____

3. _____ is a food made of dough,

   cheese, tomato sauce, and other toppings.

   _____

4. A _____ is one piece of furniture

   that might be found in a living room.

   _____

5. A _____ is someone who

   works for a newspaper. _____

6. A piece of glass that shows your reflection is

   a _____. _____

School–Home Connection

With the student, write two more words that have the schwa sound. Underline the syllable or syllables that make the schwa sound.

207

▶ **Underline the verb in each sentence. Then
rewrite the sentence in the tense shown
in parentheses ( ).**

1. The children study quietly. (past)

_____

2. The teacher will talk about the report. (past)

_____

3. Many students enjoyed music class. (present)

_____

4. Mr. Green scores the test. (future)

_____

5. Tim will hurry to school. (present)

_____

6. We play outside during recess. (past)

_____

7. You solved the math problem. (future)

_____

8. Misha practices the flute. (past)

_____

School–Home Connection

Work with your child to write three sentences
about school. Write one verb in the present
tense, one in the past tense, and one in the
future tense.

Review:
Vowel Variants:
/o͞o/oo, ew, ue, ui;
/o͝o/oo
Lesson 25

Name _____

► There are four /o͝o/ words spelled with the letters
oo and four /o͞o/ words spelled with the letters *oo*
in the word search below. Circle the words. Then
write each one in the correct column in the chart.

S	R	B	H	M	F	Q	R
P	C	O	O	K	D	J	O
B	R	O	O	K	Z	P	O
E	X	S	D	W	U	W	T
Q	D	T	O	O	T	H	V
C	A	D	R	O	O	P	A
V	P	E	N	L	W	R	D

/o͞o/	/o͝o/

School–Home Connection

With the student, think of two more words for
each column.

Practice Book
© Harcourt • Grade 3

▶ **Fold the paper along the dotted line. As each spelling word is read aloud, write it in the blank. Then unfold your paper and check your work. Practice writing any spelling words you missed.**

1. _____

2. _____

3. _____

4. _____

5. _____

6. _____

7. _____

8. _____

9. _____

10. _____

11. _____

12. _____

13. _____

14. _____

15. _____

Spelling Words

1. choose
2. booth
3. foot
4. bruise
5. threw
6. soft
7. cause
8. thaw
9. false
10. preschool
11. misspell
12. indoors
13. apart
14. across
15. around

Name _____

Review
Vowel Variant /ô/:
o, au(gh), aw, a(l),
ough

Lesson 25

Circle the word in each sentence that has the /ô/ sound. Then fill in the crossword puzzle with the words.

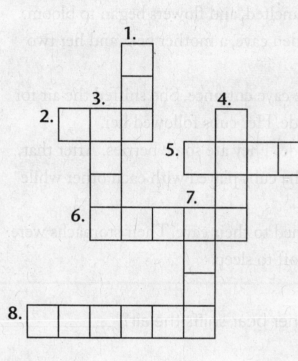

Across

2. Did you hear the crow caw?

5. What is your favorite song?

6. Bike riders ought to wear helmets.

8. The coach taught us to shoot baskets.

Down

1. My jaw was sore after I visited the dentist.

3. Kyle is my brother and also my best friend.

4. I lost my favorite ring.

7. The man told his dog to halt.

Practice Book
© Harcourt • Grade 3

▶ **Read the story. Then answer the questions about the sequence of events.**

Spring had come. The snow melted, and flowers began to bloom. The air was warm. In a cozy, hidden cave, a mother bear and her two cubs woke up.

The mother bear went to the cave entrance. She sniffed the air for danger. Then she lumbered outside. Her cubs followed her.

The bears spent all day outside. They ate some berries. After that, they splashed in the cold river. The cubs played with each other while their mother watched.

As night fell, the bears returned to their cave. Their stomachs were full. They were tired and drifted off to sleep.

1. What happens after the mother bear sniffs the air? _____

_____

2. What do the bears do before they splash in the river? _____

_____

3. What is the last thing the bears do? _____

_____

4. What time-order words and phrases are in the story? _____

_____

212

Practice Book
© Harcourt • Grade 3

Name _____

▶ **Read this part of a student's rough draft. Then answer the questions that follow.**

> (1) Mia and Simon writing a story. (2) The story are about a robot. (3) The robot is funny. (4) It _____ say all sorts of things. (5) The children are excited. (6) They will show the story to their teacher.

1. Which sentence has a singular subject and the correct form of the verb *be*?
   A Sentence 2
   B Sentence 3
   C Sentence 5
   D Sentence 6

2. Which sentence has a plural subject and the correct form of the verb *be*?
   A Sentence 2
   B Sentence 3
   C Sentence 5
   D Sentence 6

3. Which sentence has a form of the verb *be* that does NOT agree with the subject?
   A Sentence 2
   B Sentence 3
   C Sentence 5
   D Sentence 6

4. Which helping verb should go before the main verb in Sentence 1?
   A have
   B will
   C can
   D are

5. Which helping verb could complete Sentence 4?
   A have
   B had
   C can
   D is

6. Which other helping verb could replace *will* in Sentence 6?
   A had
   B can
   C have
   D were

213

Name _____

▶ Add *pre-, mis-,* or *in-* to each root word to form
a real word. Write the new word on the line.

1. exact _____

2. heat _____

3. trust _____

4. direct _____

5. behave _____

6. school _____

7. correct _____

8. read _____

9. view _____

10. match _____

School-Home Connection

Have the student explain how the prefix
changes the meaning of each root word.

214

Practice Book
© Harcourt • Grade 3

Name _____

▶ **Read the article. Circle the letter of the best answer to each question. Then write the author's message.**

You are used to getting a letter one or two days after it was mailed. In 1860, though, it could take months for your mail to arrive. That changed when the Pony Express started. It took the Pony Express only ten days to get mail from Missouri to California. Riders on horseback sped across the country with the mail. The riders faced many dangers on the trip, such as rough trails, bad weather, and robberies by bandits. The Pony Express stopped running in 1861 when a telegraph system was built. It connected the entire country. Even though the Pony Express lasted only eighteen months, it was an important way to carry mail across the country.

1. What did the Pony Express carry?

    A ponies

    B mail

    C e-mail

2. What was a danger Pony Express riders faced?

    A bad weather

    B lack of food

    C closed roads

3. What is the author's message?

_____

_____

_____

Practice Book
© Harcourt • Grade 3

Name _____

▶ **Part A.** Read each sentence. Write the Vocabulary Word from the box that is a synonym for the underlined word.

> required   inhabitants   ample
> functional   amazement   responsibility

1. The old microwave oven is barely <u>working</u>.

   _____

2. There is <u>enough</u> work to keep everyone busy.

   _____

3. Three eggs are <u>needed</u> for this recipe.

   _____

4. My biggest <u>task</u> is to take care of my little sister.

   _____

5. The firefighters made sure all the <u>residents</u> of the building got out

   safely. _____

6. Juan jumped up in <u>surprise</u> when he was named the winner.

   _____

▶ **Part B.** On a separate sheet of paper, write a sentence describing three *responsibilities* you have at home.

 School–Home Connection

Ask the student to list some of the *inhabitants* of the White House.

216

Practice Book
© Harcourt • Grade 3

▶ **Follow the path from START to FINISH. Shade in the boxes that have a word with the schwa sound. Then answer the questions.**

START	about	door	really	calmly	happy	begin
falling	happen	support	nosy	tick	scared	ray
stag	game	alarm	dentist	reckon	carrot	chorus
cast	green	taken	polite	select	gave	**FINISH**

1. Which words on the path spell the schwa sound with *a*?

   _____

2. Which words on the path spell the schwa sound with *e*?

   _____

3. Which words on the path spell the schwa sound with *o*?

   _____

4. Which words on the path spell the schwa sound with *u*?

   _____

School–Home Connection
With the student, make up three sentences
that each have two of the schwa words.

217

Practice Book
© Harcourt • Grade 3

▶ **Read this part of a student's rough draft. Then answer the questions that follow.**

> (1) William loves space. (2) He looked at pictures of the sun and moon when he was younger. (3) Now he read books about the solar system. (4) He will learn about the planets. (5) He will studies space travel. (6) One day he will become an astronaut.

1. Which sentence has a correct past-tense verb?
   A Sentence 1
   B Sentence 2
   C Sentence 4
   D Sentence 5

2. Which sentence has a correct present-tense verb?
   A Sentence 1
   B Sentence 2
   C Sentence 3
   D Sentence 4

3. Which sentence has an incorrect form of a future-tense verb?
   A Sentence 2
   B Sentence 4
   C Sentence 5
   D Sentence 6

4. Which verb should end with an *s*?
   A *looked* (Sentence 2)
   B *read* (Sentence 3)
   C *learn* (Sentence 4)
   D *become* (Sentence 6)

5. Which is the future-tense form of the verb in Sentence 1?
   A love
   B will love
   C will loves
   D loved

6. Which is the past-tense form of the verb in Sentence 4?
   A learn
   B learns
   C can learn
   D learned

Name _____

▶ **Read the article below. Write the answer to each question.**

> Winter is the time when people catch more colds. There are many reasons why people get sick more often in the winter. Children are back in school, sharing germs. The colder weather keeps grown-ups indoors, too. The nearer people are to one another, the more likely they are to spread germs. So what can you do when winter comes? Wash, wash, wash your hands. This gets rid of the germs that get on your hands. If someone is sick, stay away from him or her. And do not share food or drinks.

1. What are two causes of getting sick in the winter?

_____

_____

_____

2. What is the effect of washing your hands?

_____

3. What are two other ways to avoid getting sick?

_____

_____

School-Home Connection

Discuss with the student two cause-and-effect relationships connected to going to work or school and catching colds.

219

Practice Book
© Harcourt • Grade 3

Name _____

▶ **Read the homophones. Then complete each sentence with the correct word.**

1. (pair, pear)   I wore my favorite _____ of jeans today.

   The _____ was ripe.

2. (be, bee)   The buzzing _____ landed near Jane.

   I hope I will _____ fast enough to win

   the race.

3. (feat, feet)   Tonya's _____ were sore after

   the hike.

   The acrobat performed an amazing

   _____ of strength.

4. (horse, hoarse)   Shouting so loudly made me _____.

   Kari rode her _____ every afternoon.

5. (beat, beet)   I had a _____ salad for lunch.

   Our team _____ theirs in the final game.

6. (peak, peek)   Wait until we get to the mountain_____.

   Did you _____ at your present?

School–Home Connection

With the student, think of another sentence
for each homophone and then share the
sentences with each other.

220

Practice Book
© Harcourt • Grade 3

Name _____

▶ **Read the Spelling Words. Sort the words and write them where they belong.**

Words with -tion

1. _____

2. _____

3. _____

4. _____

5. _____

6. _____

7. _____

8. _____

9. _____

10. _____

11. _____

12. _____

13. _____

Spelling Words

1. section
2. caution
3. fiction
4. nation
5. action
6. vision
7. vacation
8. motion
9. question
10. mention
11. station
12. attention
13. portion
14. collection
15. session

Words with -sion

14. _____

15. _____

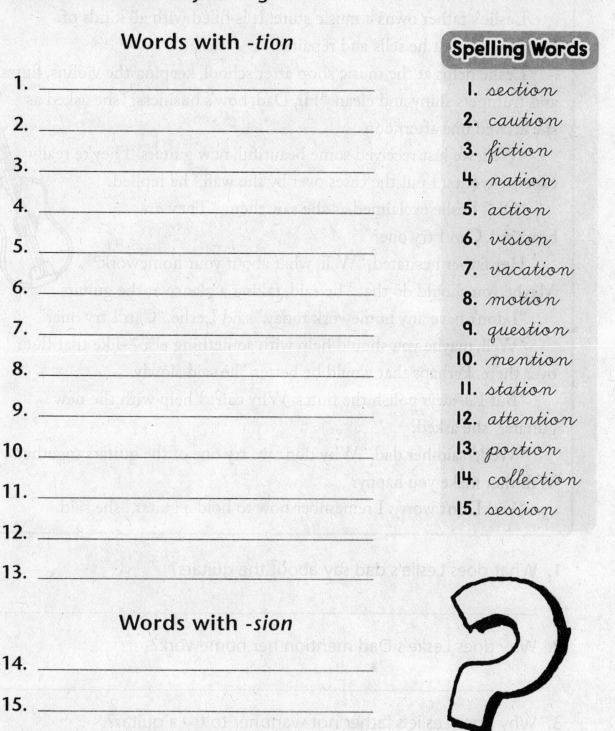

School–Home Connection

Write the words *operate* and *discuss* on a sheet of paper. Ask your child to rewrite each word adding the correct suffix. Discuss the changes in spelling and meaning that occurred.

Practice Book
© Harcourt • Grade 3

▶ **Read the story. Then answer the questions.**

Leslie's father owns a music store. It is filled with all kinds of instruments that he sells and repairs.

Leslie helps at the music shop after school, keeping the violins, flutes, and trumpets shiny and clean. "Hi, Dad, how's business?" she asked as she arrived one afternoon.

"Well, we just received some beautiful, new guitars. They're really expensive ones. I put the cases over by the wall," he replied.

"Oh!" Leslie exclaimed as she saw them. "They *are* beautiful. Can I try one?"

Her father hesitated. "Well, what about your homework? Maybe you should do that," he said, taking a glance at the guitars.

"I don't have any homework today," said Leslie. "Can I try one?"

"Well, maybe you should help with something else—like that flute over there. Perhaps that would be better," he said slowly.

"But I *always* polish the flutes. Why can't I help with the new guitars?" she asked.

"Well," said her dad. "Why don't we try one of the guitars together. Will that make you happy?"

"Yes! Don't worry. I remember how to hold a guitar," she said.

1. What does Leslie's dad say about the guitars?

   _____

2. Why does Leslie's Dad mention her homework?

   _____

3. Why does Leslie's father not want her to try a guitar?

   _____

School–Home Connection

Help the student suggest another reason why
Leslie's dad might not want her to try a guitar.

222

Name _____

▶ **Complete each sentence. Combine a root from
the box with -*tion* or -*sion* to make the missing word.**

quest_____	inject_____	object_____
collect_____	affect_____	act_____

1. It is important to take _____ to help protect

   manatees.

2. Do you have any _____ to riding in the back seat of

   a car?

3. He has a small _____ of sea shells.

4. A hug is a form of _____.

5. Dr. Harris gave the patient an _____.

6. Do you have a _____ for the guest speaker?

School–Home Connection

Have the student write sentences with the
following words: *session, affection,* and
admission.

223

Name _____

▶ **Complete the sentence about each
Vocabulary Word.**

1. If someone is _____, he or she is a **nuisance**.

_____

2. Someone who _____ is **boasting**.

_____

3. Trees move _____ when they **sway**.

_____

4. If you **oblige** someone, you make them feel as if you _____.

_____

5. If you are **summoning** someone, you are _____.

_____

6. If a dog is **sedentary**, it _____.

_____

School–Home Connection

Have the student think of different things he or
she can do to *oblige* a family member and make
a list of these things.

224

▶ As you read "Charlotte's Web," fill in the graphic organizer. Then answer the questions below.

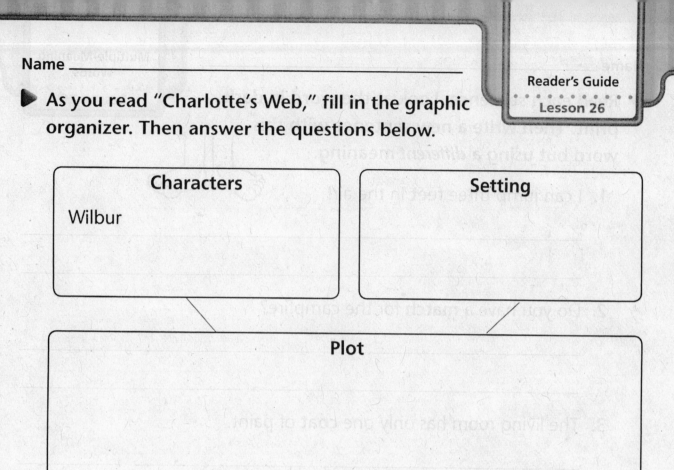

Characters

Wilbur

Setting

Plot

1. Who are some characters in the story?

_____

_____

2. What is the setting of the story?

_____

_____

▶ On a separate sheet of paper, summarize the selection. Use the graphic organizer to help you.

Practice Book
© Harcourt • Grade 3

▶ **Read each sentence. Look at the word in dark print. Then write a new sentence with this word but using a *different* meaning.**

1. I can jump three **feet** in the air!

   _____

   _____

2. Do you have a **match** for the campfire?

   _____

   _____

3. The living room has only one **coat** of paint.

   _____

   _____

4. The math and science **clubs** sponsor the annual science competition.

   _____

   _____

5. The **change** in weather is annoying.

   _____

   _____

6. A hand **wave** means "hello."

   _____

   _____

School–Home Connection

Help the student pick three words and come up with a list of descriptive phrases for each one. For example: *muddy feet, wooden club,* or a *friendly wave.*

Practice Book
© Harcourt • Grade 3

▶ **Read the following story. Then circle the letter of the best answer to each question.**

> Long ago in China, there were two sisters who were weavers of silk. One day a lady, followed by her many servants, came to their shop. "I want a gown," she said. "You will each make twenty yards of your best silk. Then I will choose which I want. I will come for it in two days."
>
> The sisters, Siwo and Sun, went to work. For two days they spun silk. Again and again Sun bragged, "I am a much better worker than you!"
>
> Siwo only replied. "One must work carefully to make silk."
>
> In two days, the lady returned. As she looked at Siwo's silk, Siwo apologized, "I could only make fifteen yards of silk."
>
> "Lady," Sun interrupted, "I have made twenty-five yards of silk!"
>
> The lady looked at Sun's silk. "Siwo's silk will make the prettiest gown."

1. Which words from the story suggest that the lady is rich and important?

   A The sisters, Siwo and Sun, went to work.

   B "One must work carefully to make silk."

   C followed by her many servants

2. Which words from the story suggest that Sun is vain?

   A Again and again Sun bragged

   B "Siwo's silk will make the prettiest gown."

   C The lady looked at Sun's silk.

3. Which words from the story suggest that Siwo had made the best silk?

   A "I want a gown."

   B In two days, the lady returned.

   C "Siwo's silk will make the prettiest gown."

School-Home Connection

Have the student write two facts from the story. Then help him or her make an inference based on those two facts.

230

Practice Book

© Harcourt • Grade 3

Name _____

▶ Read the Spelling Words. Sort the words and
write them where they belong.

Words with Two Vowel Sounds in the Middle

1. _____
2. _____
3. _____
4. _____
5. _____
6. _____
7. _____
8. _____
9. _____
10. _____

Words with Two Vowel Sounds at the End

11. _____
12. _____
13. _____
14. _____
15. _____

Spelling Words

1. lion
2. dial
3. idea
4. neon
5. science
6. area
7. radio
8. quiet
9. piano
10. fluid
11. video
12. loyal
13. stereo
14. pliers
15. create

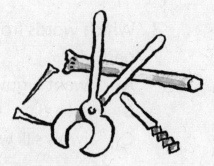

School–Home Connection

Ask your child why he or she wrote the
Spelling Words in each part of the chart.
Discuss other words that follow the same
syllable patterns.

229

Practice Book
© Harcourt • Grade 3

Name _____

► Write each word from the box next to a word
that rhymes with it. If the word has two syllables,
draw a line to show where the syllables divide.

feud	react	fuel	lead
loud	reuse	road	sour

1. rude _____

2. mode _____

3. excuse _____

4. seed _____

5. attract _____

6. jewel _____

7. crowd _____

8. power _____

School–Home Connection

Have the student write two-syllable words
that rhyme with *higher*. Then have him or her
divide those words into syllables.

231

Practice Book
© Harcourt • Grade 3

▶ **Write the letter of the Vocabulary Word that best matches each definition.**

_____ 1. an animal that is hunted for food   **A** spiral

_____ 2. a shape that curls around and around   **B** social

in a circle

_____ 3. long pieces of something   **C** reels

_____ 4. living in groups of similar animals   **D** prey

_____ 5. to wind something in   **E** shallow

_____ 6. not very deep   **F** strands

▶ **Use the graphic organizer to record facts from "Spiders and Their Webs." Fill in the box on the left with things you already know about spiders. In the box on the right, write what you learn as you read. Make inferences in the bottom box.**

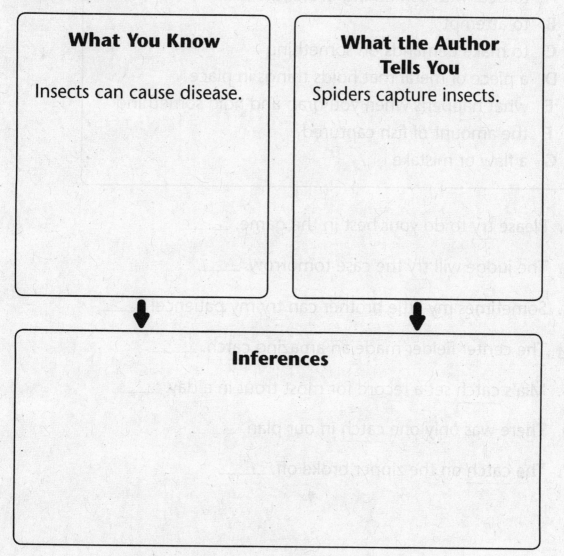

What You Know

Insects can cause disease.

What the Author Tells You

Spiders capture insects.

Inferences

▶ **On a separate sheet of paper, summarize the selection with three of your inferences. Use the graphic organizer to help you.**

Practice Book
© Harcourt • Grade 3

► Read the meanings in the box below. In each
sentence, which meaning of the underlined word
is used? Write the letter of the correct meaning on the line.

> A to deal with something in a court of law
> B to attempt
> C to make demands on something
> D a piece of metal that holds things in place
> E what happens when you grab and hold something
> F the amount of fish captured
> G a flaw or mistake

1. Please try to do your best in the game. _____

2. The judge will try the case tomorrow. _____

3. Sometimes my little brother can try my patience! _____

4. The center fielder made an amazing catch. _____

5. Mia's catch set a record for most trout in a day. _____

6. There was only one catch in our plan. _____

7. The catch on the zipper broke off. _____

School–Home Connection

Have the student use a dictionary to find at
least two meanings for the word leave.

234

Practice Book
© Harcourt • Grade 3

Name _____

▶ **Use the words in the box to complete the sentences. Then divide those words into syllables.**

appreciate	poetry	idea	biology
dial	science	violin	pliers

1. Will you _____/_____ the telephone number for me?

2. Let's think of a better _____/_____/_____.

3. Remove the nail with the _____/_____.

4. The poet writes lovely _____/_____/_____.

5. We learned about frogs in

_____/_____ class.

6. Two kinds of science are chemistry and

_____/_____/____/_____.

7. She started taking _____/____/_____ lessons

when she was five years old.

8. I_____/_____/_____/_____

that you came for a visit.

School–Home Connection
Have the student write a sentence that includes one V/V word. Then have him or her divide that word into syllables.

235

Practice Book
© Harcourt • Grade 3

Name _____

▶ **Write the adverb in each sentence. Then write the verb that it describes.**

1. My teacher talks excitedly about science.

   _____

2. Tomorrow we will learn about insects.

   _____

3. Of all the students, Evan studied the longest.

   _____

4. I speak more softly than the other students at the library.

   _____

▶ **Rewrite each sentence. Complete it with an adverb that answers the question in parentheses ( ).**

5. This spider crawls _____ than that spider. (How?)

   _____

6. I put my report _____. (Where?)

   _____

7. _____ you will learn about the sun. (When?)

   _____

236

Name _____

▶ **Read the Spelling Words. Sort the words and write them where they belong.**

Words with -*able*

1. _____

2. _____

3. _____

4. _____

Words with -*ible*

5. _____

6. _____

Words with -*less*

7. _____

8. _____

9. _____

10. _____

11. _____

Words with -*ous*

12. _____   14. _____

13. _____   15. _____

Spelling Words

1. doable
2. famous
3. careless
4. various
5. endless
6. reliable
7. nervous
8. useless
9. flexible
10. washable
11. helpless
12. terrible
13. valuable
14. dangerous
15. powerless

School–Home Connection

Make a list of additional words with the suffixes -*able*, -*ible*, -*less*, and -*ous* that you and your child can recall. Discuss the correct spellings with your child.

237

▶ **Read the story. Then answer the questions.**

"But it's vacation!" cried Nick. "I don't want to go visit Uncle James!"

"You've never even met him," Dad said. "He's a very interesting person."

Two weeks later, Nick and his father were staring at Uncle James's big old house in the country. "His house looks creepy," grumbled Nick.

Dad only smiled. "Uncle James has some unusual things. He might even show you his special trunk!"

"Who cares about an old trunk," Nick muttered.

Suddenly, a very small, elderly man opened the door. "So this must be Nick," said Uncle James. "You look just like your Uncle Phil. He was a famous mountain climber. He climbed every tall peak in North America."

"Wow," said Nick. He was impressed that he had a famous relative.

After dinner, Uncle James opened up an old trunk. In it were pictures, letters, and even newspaper articles. One by one, Uncle James introduced Nick to relatives from long ago. There were cowhands, sea captains, and even his Aunt Emma, who had lived to be 106.

---

1. What does Nick say about Uncle James in the beginning of the story?

_____

2. What is your prediction for what will happen next?

_____

_____

3. Which story clue helped you make a prediction?

_____

_____

_____

School–Home Connection

Have the student tell you an ending that will
be appropriate for the story.

238

Practice Book

© Harcourt • Grade 3

▶ **Complete the story by adding *-able* or *-ible* to each unfinished word.**

It was Aunt Marta's birthday, and Celia wanted to give her the best birthday party poss_____. She baked a cake and invited all of Aunt Marta's friends and family. Then she put on some suit_____ clothes. As she was dressing, though, Marta heard a terr_____ racket. When she looked out the window, she saw her three little brothers playing instruments. They were very aud_____, even through the window. But the music they made was laugh_____! It sounded more like a lot of banging and screeching than actual music. Still, Marta thought, her brothers might be train_____.

For the next hour, Marta helped her little brothers learn a song. They practiced hard. "Who says little kids are not teach_____?" she said to herself over and over again.

Later, at Aunt Marta's birthday dinner, the three brothers played "Happy Birthday" for Aunt Marta and all of the guests.

"Wow," everyone said when it was over. "This celebration is incred_____!"

School–Home Connection

Have the student make up a new sentence for each completed word. (For example: *It is not possible for me to fly through the air like a bird.*)

239

Practice Book
© Harcourt • Grade 3

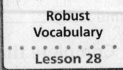
▶ **Circle the word that correctly completes each sentence.**

1. The chef _____ pepper on the salad.

   expand   sprinkled   erupt

2. The scientist did careful and _____ research on volcanoes.

   grainy   thorough   deliberation

3. The soup looked _____ and lumpy.

   erupt   sprinkled   grainy

4. The team will _____ if more people join.

   expand   deliberation   thorough

5. The jury reached its decision after a long _____.

   sprinkled   thorough   deliberation

6. That volcano may _____ soon.

   thorough   grainy   erupt

School–Home Connection

Have the student write short definitions for each Vocabulary Word.

240

Practice Book
© Harcourt • Grade 3

▶ **Realistic fiction has details that help you make predictions about events to come. You can read ahead to revise or confirm your predictions.**

Beginning

Prediction:

Look at the pictures and read pages 358–359. Use details to make a prediction about what will happen next.

↓

Middle

Confirm/Revise Prediction:

New Prediction:

Look at the pictures and read pages 361–368. Confirm your prediction.

↓

End

Confirm/Revise Prediction:

Look at the pictures and read pages 369–370. Revise or confirm your prediction. Make a new prediction about what will happen next.

▶ **On a separate sheet of paper, write a summary of "The Science Fair."**

Name _____

▶ **Read each homograph and its two pronunciations.
Write the letter of the pronunciation that goes
with each sentence.**

close	a. klōs	b. klōz	tear	c. ter	d. tir
lead	e. led	f. lēd	does	g. duz	h. dōz
wind	i. wind	j. wīnd			

1. The **wind** blew the papers down the street. _____

2. Please do not **tear** my paper. _____

3. The mother hen will **lead** her chicks to the pond. _____

4. Two **does** and two fawns drank from the river. _____

5. Did you remember to **close** the door? _____

6. I felt sad, and a **tear** came to my eye. _____

7. Frida has to **wind** her alarm clock every evening. _____

8. **Does** anyone know where my pencil is? _____

9. A kite made of **lead** will never fly. _____

10. My friend lives very **close** to me. _____

School-Home Connection
Have the student state the definition of a
homograph in his or her own words.

242

Practice Book
© Harcourt • Grade 3

Name _____

▶ **Each underlined word has the wrong suffix.
Rewrite the words with the correct suffixes.
Use** -able, -ible, -less **or** -ous.

1. The clothes that I bought today are <u>washless</u>.

   _____

2. Is that paintbrush still <u>usous</u>?

   _____

3. Those circus acrobats are <u>flexous</u>!

   _____

4. The movie was so long it seemed <u>endible</u>.

   _____

5. If you are <u>relyous</u>, I will let you borrow this CD.

   _____

6. Try not to be so <u>nerveable</u> when you perform.

   _____

7. It is too <u>dangerable</u> to ride your bike down that hill.

   _____

8. Mona was bored and <u>restable</u>.

   _____

Practice Book
© Harcourt • Grade 3

Name _____

▶ **Rewrite each sentence. Replace each contraction with the words used to form it.**

1. Alice doesn't see that we're waving.

   _____

2. She's worried that we haven't arrived.

   _____

3. I'm glad that you didn't stay home.

   _____

4. It isn't clear that he's the winner.

   _____

▶ **If the sentence is correct, write** *correct*. **If it is not, rewrite it correctly.**

5. Wouldn't you like any help?

   _____

6. I don't see my teacher nowhere.

   _____

7. There wasn't nobody in the cafeteria.

   _____

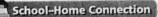

School–Home Connection

Work with your child to write three sentences
about his or her day, using contractions. Use at
least one contraction with a pronoun and one
with *not*.

244

Practice Book
© Harcourt • Grade 3

Name _____

▶ **Read the Spelling Words. Sort the words and write them where they belong.**

Words with *bi-*

1. _____
2. _____
3. _____

Words with *non-*

4. _____
5. _____
6. _____
7. _____

Words with *over-*

8. _____
9. _____
10. _____
11. _____
12. _____
13. _____
14. _____
15. _____

Spelling Words

1. overnight
2. bicycle
3. nonstop
4. overdue
5. overlook
6. biweekly
7. overflow
8. nonsense
9. oversee
10. overhead
11. nonfiction
12. overcoat
13. nonfat
14. overdone
15. biplane

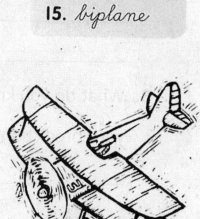

School–Home Connection

With your child, write sentences using each Spelling Word. Discuss how the prefixes *bi-*, *non-*, and *over-* change the meaning of each base word.

245

Name _____

▶ **Read the story. Then answer each question about it.**

> Vanessa and Keisha were walking home through the park. They were busy chatting, and they paid no attention to where they were. Just beyond the swings, there was a soccer field. Suddenly a strange-looking object landed right in the middle of it. It made no sound, and the girls were too busy to notice anyway. They just kept walking and talking. Then, just as they were almost past the strange object, voices began to come from it.
>
> "Do you hear something?" Vanessa asked.

1. What will happen next?

_____

_____

_____

2. What story clues helped you make your prediction?

_____

_____

_____

3. What do you know from your experience that helped you make your prediction?

_____

_____

_____

School-Home Connection

Read the story with the student. Then work together to write an ending. Be sure to point out story clues that helped you make your predictions.

Practice Book
© Harcourt • Grade 3

Name _____

▶ **Write a word from the box to complete each sentence.**

overcoat	biweekly	nonstop	overflow
nonfiction	overnight	biplane	bicycle

1. My little brother runs around _____.

2. The old _____ flies very slowly.

3. The _____ she wore over her dress was long

   and very warm.

4. Gia prefers fiction to _____.

5. We will stay _____ at the campground.

6. That magazine comes out _____, or every

   two weeks.

7. The river began to _____ its banks.

8. Tara's _____ has narrow tires.

School–Home Connection

Ask the student to explain how he or she knew
which word to use in each sentence.

Practice Book
© Harcourt • Grade 3

Name _____

▶ **Use a Vocabulary Word to complete each sentence.**

rotates	steady	reflects
surface	evidence	appears

1. We see the moon at night because it _____ light from

   the sun.

2. All the _____ suggested that he had not discovered a

   new planet.

3. When you spin the classroom globe, it _____ around

   and around.

4. My mom held the ladder _____ so Aunt Nita could

   paint the ceiling.

5. That little dog _____ to be frightened by the storm.

6. The _____ of that table is smooth.

School-Home Connection

Have the student act out the words *rotates*
and *steady*.

248

Practice Book
© Harcourt • Grade 3

Name _____

▶ Use the graphic organizer to record what you already know about the planets. Put this information under *What I Know*. Then ask questions for what you want to know about the planets. Put the questions under *What I Want to Know*. After reading, write what you have learned from "The Planets" under *What I Learned*.

What I Know	What I Want to Know	What I Learned
In the sky, there are planets, stars, a sun, and a moon.	How is a planet different from a star?	A planet is seen because the sun shines on it. A star gives off its own light.

▶ On a separate sheet of paper, summarize the selection, providing facts you have learned about the planets. Use the graphic organizer to help you.

249

Name _____

▶ **Read each sentence. Then draw a line to match the underlined homograph with the correct definition.**

1. A gray <u>dove</u> sat in the tree.

the past tense of dive

a type of bird

2. Tim sings <u>bass</u> in our chorus.

a type of fish

a voice with a deep sound

3. My sister will <u>polish</u> her trumpet.

to shine

relating to the country of Poland

4. We will <u>present</u> a gift to our teacher.

to give in a formal way

a gift

5. Temperatures were very hot out on the sandy <u>desert</u>.

a land area without water

to flee or run away

School–Home Connection

Have the student write sentences for the homographs that were not used in sentences on this page.

250

Practice Book
© Harcourt • Grade 3

▶ **Draw a line to match each word on the left with its meaning on the right. Then write sentences for three of the words.**

1. nonsense	to extend too far
2. overripe	able to use two languages
3. overextend	not sticking
4. nonstick	too ripe
5. bilingual	without sense
6. bilevel	having two levels
7. nonpayment	every two hundred years
8. overqualified	being more qualified than necessary
9. bicentennial	not paying
10. bicoastal	having to do with two seacoasts

11. _____

12. _____

13. _____

School-Home Connection

Have the student make up a sentence with at least two of the prefixed words from above. (For example: *I cooked the overripe apples in a nonstick pan.*)

Practice Book
© Harcourt • Grade 3

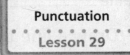

▶ **Rewrite each sentence correctly.**

1. sometimes i sing my favorite song.

_____

2. that song is called twinkle, twinkle, little star.

_____

3. those three stars are named altair castor and polaris.

_____

4. sirius is the brightest star in the sky and i see it at night.

_____

5. you can read about stars in a magazine called Ask.

_____

6. mrs. wong reads to children at the library in middletown.

_____

7. she lives in new york but she works in connecticut.

_____

8. today she reads the book a child's introduction to the night sky.

_____

_____

School–Home Connection

Write three sentences. One should include a
comma, one a title, and one a pronoun. Read
them aloud, and challenge your child to write
them down correctly.

Practice Book
© Harcourt • Grade 3

Name _____

▶ **Part A. Add** -*tion* **or** -*sion* **to the following root words.**

1. omit _____

2. infect _____

3. explode _____

4. celebrate _____

5. decide _____

▶ **Part B. Use the words you wrote in Part A to complete the following sentences.**

6. When the fireworks went off, they made a loud

_____.

7. Choosing a present for someone can be a difficult

_____.

8. We had a _____ for my sister's high school

graduation.

9. Emily is at home with an ear _____.

10. The _____ of two letters on the sign made it

very confusing!

School–Home Connection

Have the student tell the meanings of each of the new words. Tell him or her to check with a dictionary if necessary.

253

Practice Book
© Harcourt • Grade 3

Name _____

▶ Fold the paper along the dotted line. As each
spelling word is read aloud, write it in the blank.
Then unfold your paper, and check your work.
Practice writing any spelling words you missed.

1. _____

2. _____

3. _____

4. _____

5. _____

6. _____

7. _____

8. _____

9. _____

10. _____

11. _____

12. _____

13. _____

14. _____

15. _____

Spelling Words

1. vision
2. caution
3. session
4. fluid
5. piano
6. loyal
7. reliable
8. flexible
9. powerless
10. dangerous
11. famous
12. biplane
13. nonstop
14. overnight
15. oversee

► **Look at each row of words. Underline the word that has the V/V syllable pattern. Then use it in a sentence on the line below. Divide the V/V word into syllables.**

1. laid   out   fuel

_____

2. loud   science   flies

_____

3. react   road   does

_____

4. lies   tried   cereal   meat

_____

5. diary   dairy   lead

_____

School–Home Connection

For each word, have the student write another word in which the same letters make the same V/V sound.

255

▶ **Read the story. Then write your answers to the questions on the lines below.**

Aida dropped her bag and sat down. Her face was bright red, and she wiped the sweat off her forehead.

"Aida, what's wrong?" asked her brother Tim.

Aida poured a glass of water and drank it all. "Coach Lee made us do four extra laps!"

Tim dropped a few ice cubes into Aida's glass. "Sounds like the new coach is really tough on the team."

"We're getting ready for the big game next week," Aida replied. She leaned her head back and closed her eyes.

"Are you nervous?" asked Tim.

"No, not yet," said Aida.

1. How do you think Aida feels? How can you tell?

_____

_____

_____

2. How do you think Tim feels about Aida?

_____

_____

3. How do you think Aida will feel on the day of her big game? Why?

_____

_____

_____

 School–Home Connection

Have the student tell you the facts that
helped him or her answer these questions. For
example, Aida is tired because she is sweating.

Practice Book
© Harcourt • Grade 3

▶ **Read this part of a student's rough draft. Then answer the questions that follow.**

> (1) Yesterday my class went to an animal park. (2) We saw lions from the window of the school bus. (3) One lion _____ on a rock. (4) Monkeys played happily in the trees. (5) Some of them <u>come</u> excitedly to the bus. (6) _____, I will write a story about all the animals I seen.

1. Which of these verb forms could go in the blank in Sentence 3?
   A sit
   B sets
   C sat
   D set

2. Which verb needs the helping verb *have* before it?
   A went (Sentence 1)
   B saw (Sentence 2)
   C write (Sentence 6)
   D seen (Sentence 6)

3. Which is the past-tense form that could replace the underlined verb in Sentence 5?
   A comes
   B comed
   C came
   D camed

4. Which sentence has an adverb that tells *when*?
   A Sentence 1
   B Sentence 2
   C Sentence 4
   D Sentence 5

5. Which sentence does NOT have an adverb?
   A Sentence 1
   B Sentence 2
   C Sentence 4
   D Sentence 5

6. Which adverb could go in the blank in Sentence 6?
   A Tomorrow
   B More quickly
   C Most slowly
   D More slow

▶ **Underline the word with a prefix in each sentence. Then write its meaning on the line.**

1. Our bicoastal flight from New York to California took five and a half hours.

   _____

2. Billy took all nonessential items out of his backpack.

   _____

3. None of the overhead lights was on when we got home.

   _____

4. Mareeka made a face when she took a bite of the overripe banana.

   _____

5. What Trina said was nonsense, so we did not believe her.

   _____

6. The bilevel house is the biggest on our street.

   _____

Practice Book
© Harcourt • Grade 3

Name _____

▶ **Read each sentence. Then choose the sentence that uses the same meaning for the underlined word. Circle the letter of the best answer.**

1. Please <u>lay</u> those bags down carefully.

   A Chickens can lay more than three hundred eggs per year.

   B John will lay his clothes out on his bed.

2. Whom did you <u>pick</u> to play on your kickball team?

   A Mom let me pick what we had for dinner last night.

   B We will pick flowers from our garden to put on the table.

3. It is hard to <u>tie</u> a butterfly knot.

   A Do not forget to tie your shoes before you leave.

   B Gina scored a basket to tie the game.

4. I used <u>tape</u> to fix my torn paper.

   A Please put the tape in the VCR.

   B Herman attached the picture to the wall with tape.

5. The leaves change color in the <u>fall</u>.

   A The ice skater's fall looked painful.

   B Do you prefer fall or winter?

6. Dan took a <u>trip</u> to the park.

   A I would like to go on a hiking trip.

   B A trip over loose wires can cause a sprained ankle.

School–Home Connection

Ask the student to write a sentence that uses
the second meaning of *fall* from #5.

259

Name _____

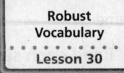

▶ **Part A. Draw a line to match each Vocabulary Word with its definition.**

1. observed   a. to keep safe

2. confirm   b. to make bigger

3. magnify   c. creates or makes

4. picturesque   d. to make sure

5. generates   e. looked at closely

6. safeguard   f. like a picture

▶ **Part B. Write answers to the questions on the lines below.**

7. What are three ways you could confirm that it was snowing outside?

_____

_____

8. If you observed a bird's nest for a day, what might you see?

_____

_____

School–Home Connection

Ask the student to name a place where he or
she might find a machine that *generates* snow.

260

Practice Book
© Harcourt • Grade 3

Name _____

▶ **Use the clues to complete the puzzle. Use words with suffixes.**

ACROSS
1. capable of being relied upon
4. capable of being reached
7. full of fame
8. without power

DOWN
2. without end
3. capable of being worn
5. full of humor
6. capable of being done

Practice Book
© Harcourt • Grade 3

▶ **Read this part of a student's rough draft. Then answer the questions that follow.**

> (1) Latisha, Latisha's father and his friend went to Tonto National Forest in Arizona. (2) They _____ stay long but they had a great time. (3) They camped, hiked and swam on friday. (4) On Saturday night they sang a song around the campfire called "Make New Friends." (5) Latisha didn't never want to leave the forest.

1. Which sentence has a contraction?

  A Sentence 1

  B Sentence 3

  C Sentence 4

  D Sentence 5

2. Which contraction could go in the blank in Sentence 2?

  A doesn't

  B aren't

  C couldn't

  D they're

3. Which sentence has a double negative that needs to be corrected?

  A Sentence 1

  B Sentence 3

  C Sentence 4

  D Sentence 5

4. Which of these sentences does NOT need a comma added?

  A Sentence 1

  B Sentence 2

  C Sentence 3

  D Sentence 5

5. Which of these sentences has a proper noun that is incorrect?

  A Sentence 1

  B Sentence 3

  C Sentence 4

  D Sentence 5

6. Which sentence is correct?

  A Sentence 1

  B Sentence 3

  C Sentence 4

  D Sentence 5

Name _____

▶ **Read the story. Then write your answer to each question.**

Ravi swung the bat again and missed. "I'm never going to hit the ball!" he cried, stomping his feet.

"Just keep your eye on it," his sister said.

"I am keeping my eye on the ball!" Ravi yelled.

"You have to relax. Close your eyes and take a deep breath."

Ravi put his bat down and closed his eyes. He breathed in deeply and smelled the fresh grass and the trees.

"Now think of me throwing the ball. You see it coming slowly. Now you hit the ball. It flies into left field. Ready?"

Ravi nodded and opened his eyes. He took a few practice swings. His sister threw him the ball.

---

1. What is Ravi's problem in the story?

_____

_____

2. What does Ravi do to solve his problem?

_____

_____

3. What do you think will happen next in the story? Why?

_____

_____

School–Home Connection
Have the student write a paragraph that
continues the story.

Practice Book
© Harcourt • Grade 3

Name _____

▶ **Read each sentence. Then write a second sentence, using a different meaning of the underlined homograph.**

1. John plays the <u>bass</u> guitar in a band.

   _____

   _____

2. There is an empty desk at the end of the <u>row</u>.

   _____

   _____

3. My father loves to listen to his old <u>records</u>.

   _____

   _____

4. There is a <u>tear</u> in my jacket.

   _____

   _____

5. I <u>object</u> to having too much homework over the winter holiday.

   _____

   _____

6. I do not want to <u>subject</u> you to such a sad event.

   _____

   _____

School–Home Connection

Make a homograph glossary with the student,
using the words above. Have the student write
the underlined word and then the definitions
for both meanings.

264

Index

COMPREHENSION

GRAMMAR

Practice Book

© Harcourt • Grade 3

Irregular verbs 228, 260

Main and helping verbs 192, 216

Past-tense and future-tense verbs 208, 210

Present-tense verbs 200, 210

The verb *be* 184, 216

LITERARY RESPONSE AND ANALYSIS

Characters and setting 2, 10, 41

Plot 90, 98, 124

Theme 150, 158, 169

PHONICS

Accented and unaccented syllables 207, 220

C-*le* syllable 91, 95, 121

Compound words 47, 51, 77

Consonant blends: *str, scr, spr* 71, 75, 88

Consonant digraphs: /ch/*ch, tch*; /sh/*sh, ch*; /(h)w/*wh* 55, 59, 82

Consonant digraphs: /n/*kn, gn*; /r/*wr*; /f/*gh* 99, 103, 123

Consonants: /s/*c*; /j/*g, dge* 107, 111, 126

CVC*e*, CVVC pattern 23, 36

CVC pattern 7, 33

Diphthongs: /ou/*ou, ow*; /oi/ *oi, oy* 63, 67, 80

Plurals: *-s, -es* 27, 44

Prefixes: *bi-, non-, over-* 247, 251, 264

Prefixes: *pre-, mis-, in-* 195, 199, 212

Prefixes: *un-, re-, dis-* 159, 163, 176

r-controlled vowel: /ôr/*or, ore, our, oar, ar* 135, 139, 165

r-controlled vowel: /ûr/*er, ir, ur, or, ear* 143, 147, 170

Root word + ending: *-ed, -ing* 11, 15, 38

Schwa /ə/ 203, 207, 220

Short vowels: /a/*a*, /e/*e*, /i/*i*, /o/*o*, /u/*u* 3, 33

Suffixes: *-able, -ible, -less, -ous* 239, 243, 256

Suffixes: *-er, -est, -ly, -ful* 151, 155, 168

Suffixes: *-tion, -sion* 223, 227, 253

Syllable endings: *-s, -es* 31, 44

VCCCV pattern in longer words 7, 33

VCCCV syllable pattern 75, 88

V/CV and VC/V syllable patterns 115, 119, 129

Vowel digraphs: *ee, ea*; *ai, ay*; *oa, ow* 19, 36

Vowel variant/ô/: o, au(gh), aw, a(l), ough 187, 191, 211
Vowel variants: /o͞o/oo, ew, ue, ui; /o͝o/oo 179, 183, 209
V/V syllable pattern 231, 235, 255

RESEARCH AND INFORMATION SKILLS

Locate information 18, 26, 37
Use a dictionary 22, 30, 42
Use alphabetical order 6, 14, 43
Use graphic aids 110, 118, 132
Use reference sources 66, 74, 86

SPELLING

Compound words 45, 79
Consonant blends str, scr, spr, chr 69, 79
Consonant digraphs /ch/ ch, tch; /sh/ sh; /wh/ wh 53, 79
Consonant -le syllable pattern 89, 122
Consonants /s/ c, /j/ g, dge 105, 122
Long vowel digraphs /ē/ ee, ea; /ā/ ai, ay; /ō/ oa, ow 17, 35
Plurals -s, -es 25, 35
Prefixes bi-, non-, over- 245, 255
Prefixes pre-, mis-, in- 193, 211
Prefixes un-, re-, dis- 157, 167
r-controlled vowels /ir/ er, ir, ur, or, ear 141, 167
r-controlled vowels /ôr/ or, ore, our, ar 133, 167
Root word + endings -ed, -ing 9, 35
Schwa /ə/ 201, 211
Short vowels a, e, i, o, u 1, 35
Silent letters kn, gn, wr, gh 97, 122
Suffixes -able, -ible, -less, -ous 237, 255
Suffixes -er, -est, -ly, -ful 149, 167
Suffixes -tion, -sion, 221, 255
Vowel diphthongs /ou/ ou, ow; /oi/ oi, oy 61, 79
Vowel variants /ô/ o, au, aw, a(l), au(gh) 185, 211
Vowel variants /oo/ oo, ew, ue, ui; /oo/oo 177, 211
V/CV and VC/V syllable 113, 122
V/V syllable pattern 229, 255

VOCABULARY